Pill
Peddlers

Pill Peddlers:

Essays on the History of the Pharmaceutical Industry

Jonathan Liebenau,
symposium organizer and chairman

Gregory J. Higby and Elaine C. Stroud, editors

Symposium presented at the Wellcome
Institute for the History of Medicine, London, 1987

American Institute of the History of Pharmacy
Madison, Wisconsin
1990

Publication No. 13 (New Series)
Gregory J. Higby and Elaine C. Stroud, General Editors

COVER: Trade card of Beasley and Jones, chemists at Leamington, England, from the early nineteenth century. (*The William Helfand Collection*)

An Urdang Publication
on International Trends in Pharmaceutical History

first in a series dedicated to the memory of
GEORGE URDANG
(1882–1960)

Historian of Pharmacy and Founding Director (1941–1957)
of the American Institute of the History of Pharmacy

Contents

Foreword

THE title of this book, *Pill Peddlers,* comes from an allusion to the drug industry in Sinclair Lewis's novel of 1925, *Arrowsmith.* Since two of the essays in this volume quote that passage from Lewis, as examples of the public image of the pharmaceutical industry, we thought it appropriate as a provocative title for this collection of essays. It serves as a reminder of the generally low esteem accorded the pharmaceutical industry throughout much of its history.

This book marks the beginning of the George Urdang Series on international trends in the history of pharmacy. As the first director of the American Institute of the History of Pharmacy, Urdang (1882–1960) was instrumental in bringing rigor and breadth of scope to the field in the United States. A refugee from Nazi Germany, Urdang paid special attention to the history of his adopted home without losing sight of the broader issues within pharmacy. This series will build on the tradition begun with the work he wrote fifty years ago with Edward Kremers, *History of Pharmacy.*

The first publication in the Urdang Series is the result of a symposium organized in 1987 by Jonathan Liebenau at the Wellcome Institute in London, where Dr. Liebenau brought together a group of scholars to describe and analyze the development of the pharmaceutical industry in various countries, and to suggest new areas for research. By publishing papers from that symposium, the AIHP hopes to encourage further exploration of an industry that in little more than a century grew from obscurity to predominance in the field of pharmacy.

Gregory J. Higby and Elaine C. Stroud

Introduction

by Jonathan Liebenau,
Chairman of the Symposium

THE pharmaceutical industry has been seen from a variety of points of view by social scientists who have emphasized issues such as its economic importance, its political significance, and its industrial character. It has long been recognized as a disproportionately powerful influence on the character of medicine, and supporters as well as detractors have commented on its leading role in national medical services as well as in therapeutic practice. Only recently have historians begun to pay serious attention to it. This is partly due to the conceptual difficulties in dealing with such a complexity of factors that historians wish to analyze simultaneously: the character of the industry as a whole and the activities of individual companies, the content of commercial medical science and technology, and the impact of proprietary medicines upon the medical profession; the role of governments and the conduct of business. The delay also has been due to difficulties in getting research materials. This was sometimes caused by companies themselves denying access to outsiders, but for the most part it is only recently that business archives have been properly collected, ordered, cataloged, and made available.

This volume is one of the first products of the combined willingness of historians to confront the conceptual complexities and to exploit the newly available archives. It originated in the first conference of its kind, held in January 1987 at the Wellcome Institute for the History of Medicine, London. That meeting not only stimulated the writing of most of the papers here, it also provoked a great deal of discussion about research methods and the goals of historians of the pharmaceutical industry. Two essays have been specially commissioned to cover two important areas: relations between industry and academe in the United States, and the Basel group of pharmaceutical manufacturers.

The range of that meeting, as is reflected in these papers, dealt mainly with the character of the pharmaceutical industry in various

1

national contexts. All of the major producing countries were represented, though the essay on Germany could not be included in this volume. Britain is considered from the point of view both as the major trading country in the late eighteenth and nineteenth century and as an important respondent to foreign developments. France is similarly seen as an historically important producer and a major market for medicines, as well as in the way it responded to the challenges of the leading manufacturers in Germany and Switzerland. These papers not only review what has gone on in the industry as a whole, they also trace a number of critical themes in the twentieth-century history of the industry. The relationship between the industry and the profession of pharmacology and its general links with academe are discussed in two essays. The character of individual companies is covered, as are a few exemplary research laboratories and special efforts.

The early years of the industry are described in the evocative paper by Porter and Porter, which ties the basic role of the dispensing chemist's shop to the emerging business of the large-scale pharmaceutical trader. From this essay we can easily see what the reality of business was like in the period shortly before the establishment of large firms with professional management and a complex of interrelations linking together the scientific community, the medical profession, and the business world. As these relationships slowly emerged in the early nineteenth century, each of the parties involved needed to feel their own way and to discover what relationship would serve their vaguely defined interests.

Those interests were more clearly understood by the emerging pharmaceutical manufacturers of Britain towards the end of the nineteenth century. Liebenau shows how a largely ill-formed industrial community was able to recognize its need for common purpose and, through the stimulus of a series of discreet events, was able to identify a means of responding. Such responses are characteristic of an industry groping with new opportunities and challenges. In the case of the British pharmaceutical industry, the opportunities came from a sophisticated medical profession and an advanced scientific community. Challenges came from the foreign industry, which not only threatened to dominate the British market, but also looked as though it was making British manufacturers obsolete.

The French industry was obsolete in another way. Re-formed in the nineteenth century around the principle that drugs manufacturing ought to be confined to those involved in the practice of pharmacy, the French had almost legislated against any possibility of dynamism. As Robson shows in one of the first studies of the French industry based on archives, that conservatism put it in a parlous position. Furthermore, he shows that studying the French condition is a particularly good way of gauging the effects of the German and Swiss industry upon their major export markets.

Two of the papers in this volume originated within companies. Both the chapter on the Wellcome Physiological Research Laboratories and on the growth of Sandoz within the Basel industrial community were written by company archivists. Their ready access to material, as well as their deep familiarity with their companies is apparent in their writing. These authors, it must be stressed, have been instrumental in not only ordering their collections in exemplary ways, but in allowing scholars access to them.

Reidl presents a general review of the state of affairs in Basel, where numerous fine chemical manufacturers took advantage of the excellent transportation as well as the good water afforded by the Rhine River to locate in the corner of Switzerland uniquely suitable for reaching major French and German markets, as well as serving domestic needs. Although they began quite differently, each of the three companies that resulted from the original Basel manufacturers has come to play a somewhat similar role in the structure of the multinational pharmaceutical industry. All concentrated on the advantages Switzerland and that unique local community provided, such as excellent stimulus to trade, a favorable financial climate, a high quality scientific staff, and, perhaps paradoxically, the lack of patent controls.

Tansey and Milligan show us the sequence of events and the thinking behind the establishment of a leading British pharmaceutical laboratory. The Wellcome company had been unusual from the outset in that it was strongly influenced by both the German research ideal and American marketing practices. These well-suited bedfellows combined to form one of the earliest commercial laboratories, and almost certainly the first company-sponsored pharmaceutical research institution in Britain.

The two essays on conditions in the United States concentrate on the theme of academics and industry. Swann examines the origins of the tainted image of industrial research held by American academic scientists. For clues he looks at the unique development of the system of higher education in America that took the German experience as its model. As Swann shows, the American university emerged as an amalgam of fundamental and applied research functions. Industrial leaders in the United States also looked to German models and learned that research was essential. Fueled by ideology as much as skilled manpower, these large companies invented the form of research-based product development that has come to characterize the entire modern pharmaceutical industry. Developments on both sides of the industry/academe fence eventually led the participants to see that cooperation would lead to benefits for both.

Parascandola takes a closer look at the relationship between the community of pharmaceutical scientists and manufacturers by focusing on pharmacology and the academic reluctance to admit industrial scientists into their professional society in the first half of the twentieth century. The reputation of the pharmaceutical industry was one factor in academic reluctance, as was the traditional opposition of the medical community to commercial endeavors. The fear of any taint of commercialism was perhaps more pronounced in pharmacology because of their close links with the testing of the efficacy of drugs. The newly developing discipline was cautious in distancing itself from the pharmaceutical industry, which was undergoing changes itself. Eventually the barriers were broken down as the quality of the research in American pharmaceutical companies improved and links were forged between the university researcher and the industry in the form of consultantships and collaborative efforts. This is a peculiarly American story, dealing with the professionalism of both the drug industry and the discipline of pharmacology.

This volume, then, brings together a collection of essays that will help us form an opinion of how the worldwide pharmaceutical industry came into being. In some ways it should be seen as the starting point for a new approach to the history of the pharmaceutical industry. Although eclectic in approach and varying in scope, these essays show the willingness of pharmaceutical historians to confront complex issues and to utilize company archives. As new issues are identified and new archives are made available, it is our hope that this work will be superseded. Until that happens, however, this volume will provide a guide on how to approach the history of this key industry.

The Rise of the
English Drugs Industry:
The Role of Thomas Corbyn

by Roy Porter and Dorothy Porter

REVISIONIST scholarship over the last generation has immensely sharpened our understanding of medical politics. We no longer see the history of medicine as the straightforward increase of knowledge, science, and skill; or as the rise of colleges, universities, and hospitals, all representing the evolution of a natural division of medical labor; or as the march, onwards and upwards, of professionalism.[1] Rather, thanks to the writings of Holloway, Waddington, and others, we now construe such issues as reform and professionalization as ideological footballs, kicked around by rival interest groups in endless and unresolved struggles to secure power, prestige, and livelihoods.[2]

But if medical politics has now, rightly, been spotlighted, the economics of medicine remains in the shadows. True, there have been some advances. The researches above all of Raach, Webster, and Pelling for the sixteenth and seventeenth centuries,[3] of Burnby, Holmes, Lane, and Loudon for the eighteenth,[4] and of Peterson[5] for the Victorian age have compelled us to abandon the old idea that common practitioners—as distinct from metropolitan élite physicians—long remained few and impoverished. On the contrary, in numbers, geographical distribution, skill, income, and status, general practitioners formed a major presence at least from late Tudor times onwards, and paradoxically it may have been precisely the nineteenth century which, in an overstocked market, actually saw the erosion, rather than the enhancement, of the prestige and pockets of practitioners at large.

Wellcome Institute for the History of Medicine, 183 Euston Road, London NW1 2BP, United Kingdom.

Reprinted with permission of the authors from: *Medical History* 33 (1989): 277–295. Spellings have been changed to American usage.

Even so, and despite a few pioneering studies of doctors' ledgers and bank balances,[6] our understanding of both the incomes of medical practitioners, and, still more important, of how practitioners actually built up their bank balances, guinea by guinea, remains rudimentary. Superiority to filthy lucre formed part of the ethos of the medical hierarchy, and that snobbery seems to have rubbed off on to medical historians, who have almost universally ignored the money side of medicine.

Above all, we know pitifully little about medicine's wider economic structure and networks. Many of its practices were traditionally, of course, highly individualistic, involving direct monetary exchanges between patient and practitioner. Until quite recently, to practice physic or surgery, required little capital investment in plant and equipment, nor any organized workforce. It was know-how, skill, and services, rather than commodities, which counted. The practitioner was no "corporate man"; he dealt face-to-face with his client, and not through intermediaries. In these respects, the commercial nexuses which medicine generated remained fairly simple.

But it would obviously be wrong to assume that this face-to-face model offers any complete understanding of the business of medicine. For one thing, individualism was traditionally tempered by collectivism. Guilds, companies, corporations, and colleges set the broad conditions of practice—e.g., entry into the profession—even if they impinged little upon the day-to-day livelihoods of their members.[7] Thus, in the eighteenth century, one of the informal functions of the new provincial medical societies was to fix fees, and such works as Thomas Percival's *Medical ethics* (1803) warned practitioners about the evils of price-cutting and fee wars.

Moreover, complex reciprocal ties of clientage, patronage, and mutual interdependency clearly counted for much. Practitioners from different strata had many opportunities to put business in each others' way. For example, as was alleged in a pamphlet, *The apothecaries' mirror, or the present state of pharmacy exploded* (1790),[8] physicians would commonly prescribe gallons of medicines to benefit the apothecary, who in turn would reciprocate by recommending only those physicians reputed to "write well" by "multiplying their nauseous superfluities."[9] Such devices, underneath the veneer of high ethics, must have been widespread, though we generally know about them only when they became so threatening to the public interest as to require Parliamentary intervention. Thus, in the nineteenth century, physicians who certified the insane were explicitly prohibited from accepting backhanders from the private-madhouse operators, though, as we know from the notorious practices of John Conolly, unscrupulous doctors were still tempted to ride roughshod over the law.[10]

The business of medicine should not be seen, however, simply as a matter of the sale of skills.[11] For most branches of medicine also dealt more and more in an increasingly significant commodity: drugs. A crescendo of commentators through the seventeenth and eighteenth centuries, many of them practitioners weeping crocodile tears, remarked upon, and, typically, deplored, the vast increase in the consumption of medicaments. Certainly, the supply side of the equation swelled massively between the sixteenth century and the nineteenth. Up to 1600, the materia medica remained fairly traditional, relying upon simples and the time-honored herb-based Galenicals. This changed. During the seventeenth century, the importation of drugs from the Orient and the New World soared at least twenty-five fold, and by the Restoration, several hundred kinds of exotic drugs were readily available.[12] Moreover, many of these newer items—for instance, ipecacuanha and Jesuits' Bark—proved effective and highly popular.

Other developments gave prominence to new drug remedies not available from routine kitchen physic. The Paracelsian and Van Helmontian movements in alchemy and chemistry stimulated the introduction of new mineral, metallic, and chemical medicines, making free use of such laboratory-produced ingredients as aqua fortis, calomel, antimonials, ferrous sulphate, and Glauber's salt.[13] Iatrochemistry was boosted by the founding of the Society of Chemical Physicians at the time of the Restoration. Significantly, from 1672 onwards, the Society of Apothecaries ran its own dispensary.[14] Successive versions of the *London Pharmacopoeia*—there were nine editions from 1621 to 1809—show an increasing percentage of mineral and chemical cures.

This increased supply was clearly matched by growing demand. Sick people, all agreed, were no longer satisfied with the ancient regimens recommended back in the good old days of learned physic; they now insisted upon lavish and up-to-date drug therapies.[15] Physicians blamed the change on unscrupulous apothecaries, who exploited patients' susceptibilities, and on know-all patients' inveterate itch to dose themselves.[16] Eighteenth-century moralists argued that the corruptions of civilization produced the nervous disorder they called the "English malady," which itself bred hypochondria and led to heavy drug-dependence.[17]

Whatever the cause, the reshaping of medical practice from the late seventeenth century further encouraged liberality in the use of medicines. Dispensaries for the poor, set up first at the end of the seventeenth century by the College of Physicians, and then in the late eighteenth century by lay-financed charities, clearly identified treatment with drugs.[18] The vast expansion of "irregular" medicine in the eighteenth century depended almost wholly upon the nationwide advertising, distribution, and sale of patent and proprietary nostrums in unparalleled quantities (nearly two million doses of Dr. James' Powders were sold within a twenty-year period).[19]

Possibly most important of all, from 1704 apothecaries enjoyed the legal right to give medical advice (or in effect, to practice physic), so long as they charged only for their medicines. Doubtless, it was also psychologically easier to get patients to pay for boluses or electuaries, more tangible than words. For both reasons, apothecaries' treatment became synonymous in the eyes of their detractors with over-dosing and over-charging. In the late seventeenth century, when Sir George Wheler fell sick and was treated by Sir George Ent, his apothecary's bill came to no less than £28.[20] Indeed, the Rose Case of 1703-4, which secured the apothecaries' right to prescribe, sprang from the indignation of a butcher, John Seale, when presented by his apothecary, William Rose, with a bill for his year's medicines totalling £50.[21]

Recent research has demonstrated how handsomely apothecaries benefited from a medicine boom they had helped to start. Apothecaries' spokesmen, from the time of their struggles with the College of Physicians around 1700, right through to the attempts of emergent general practitioners to secure legal recognition in the first half of the nineteenth century, liked to paint a David and Goliath picture of apothecaries, the poor, downtrodden, oppressed branch of medicine, standing as the solitary selfless guardians of the public interest against the selfish, monopolistic big guns of the Colleges.[22] Historians have been known to take this propaganda at face value.[23]

But recent research, above all by Loudon and Burnby, has amply demonstrated that from the mid-seventeenth century onwards a substantial proportion of apothecaries-cum-general practitioners were themselves basking in new prosperity and upward mobility, confirming the accuracy of Robert Campbell's statement, in his *English tradesman* (1747), that the apothecary's was a "very profitable trade. . . . His profits are unconceivable," or the thrust of a hostile pamphlet of 1748 in which "the Apothecaries' monstrous profits are exposed."[24] All the signs are that emergent general practitioners—for example, the Pulsford family of Wells in Somerset—made the most of the eighteenth-century consumer boom to increase their incomes (or to grow fat upon the public, as their enemies put it).[25] William Broderip, the Bristol apothecary, had an annual income around the end of the eighteenth century of as much as £6,000, kept a carriage and coachman, and enjoyed both a town and a country residence. He was exceptional but not unique.[26] Up and down the country, wealthy apothecaries were buying property, building houses, making good matches, and holding public office. Some enjoyed the mayoralty: Thomas Macro was five times mayor of Bury St. Edmunds. A few apothecaries, such as James St. Amand and George Bruere, even rose to become MPs.[27]

The Golden Age of the apothecary-cum-general practitioner saw him leaping over the counter, stepping into the physician's shoes, and becoming a prescriber in his own right, at the same time retaining the apothecary's traditional prerogative of dispensing. This new role, however, also carried its cost. Increasingly out visiting on his rounds, the new-style apothecary necessarily neglected his shop. Perhaps he also came to despise the counter and mere trade. Putting on airs and graces, he upped his charges. At this point, historians tell us, the old David had, in effect, turned into a Goliath who, in turn, met a new David.[28] For the apothecary's monopoly as dispenser of drugs was challenged—"usurped" was the word they used—from the last decades of the eighteenth century onwards by the sudden expansion of the numbers of shopkeeping chemists and druggists filling the vacuum. Having laid nothing out on medical training, and having no costly and time-consuming rounds to make, the druggist could profitably undercut the apothecary-cum-general practitioner when it came to selling drugs.[29]

Apothecaries represented their new rivals as ignorant interlopers, a public health hazard: for unlike apothecaries, druggists had no prescribed regular training. The apothecaries lobbied Parliament to outlaw dispensing by druggists (it was rightfully the apothecaries' prerogative), and even more urgently, to prevent unqualified druggists from prescribing. In this, as the Apothecaries' Act (1815) shows, they were unsuccessful.

In most historical accounts, chemists and druggists become visible only when country doctors, especially once organized into the General Pharmaceutical Association of Great Britain, founded in 1794, began attacking them. The historian's assumption that the apothecaries' accusations were largely justified possibly reveals an unconscious desire to cast the emergent GP in a heroic light, and a residual snobbishness about retail trade. As a result, the early history of pharmacy has been neglected, and this neglect must be harmful.

For one thing, it has surely led, as we hope to show below, to a misleading account of the nature and chronology of the drugs trade. For another, it means that our picture of the organization and interdependence—the whole economy—of medical practice has become puzzling or distorted. If, for example, as current research seems to be demonstrating, the habit of self-physick was notably more common from the late seventeenth century, it is vital to know the channels through which sick people obtained their medicines.[30] Moreover, how did physicians and apothecaries themselves obtain their drugs? How many—in 1700, 1750, or 1800—were still drying their own herbs or distilling their own essential oils? Or were the great majority increasingly buying practically all their materia medica ready-made from wholesalers and middlemen? If that was happening, druggists must thereby assume a crucial—though until now all too shadowy—role as the manufacturers and distributors of the very sinews of medicine. They become integral to that surge of large-scale manufacturing and marketing which we call the Industrial

Revolution; they become the authentic progenitors of the pharmaceutical industry.

Of course, these dimensions of the economic history of medicine may well remain hardly visible if we go on equating druggists with ignorant shopkeepers, and assuming that the retail druggist only "first appeared in the 1780s." As a recent account has phrased it, "it does seem certain that the dispensing druggist appeared and multiplied in the last two decades of the eighteenth century":

> Previously druggists were nearly always wholesalers, supplying the apothecaries. When the change occurred, however, the druggist started to supply the public with medicine sold over the counter at a much lower price than that charged by medical practitioners.[31]

Of course, there is an element of truth in this view. The trade directories indicate the swiftly increasing presence of chemists and druggists in the late eighteenth century. They suggest that many towns—Sheffield is a good example—boasted just a single druggist around 1770, perhaps six by 1800, and a dozen or two by the 1820s.[32]

Yet if our primary interest is not in title and status, nor in interprofessional rivalry between proto-general practitioners and druggists, but rather in the material economics of the medical business, it is important not to be misled by formal terminology. It is not obvious, for example, that this apparent surge in the number of pharmacy shops was real. More were listed, but this may not truly indicate a correspondingly sharp increase in premises serving as pharmacies. For one thing, it says nothing of the earlier sale of drugs by grocers and general shopkeepers. For another, it may indicate that established chemists' shops, formerly run by qualified apothecaries, were increasingly being transferred to tradesmen calling themselves "druggists." Thus one can trace the continuous existence of a pharmacy business in Derby from the mid-seventeenth century.[33] Up to 1764, the premises were run by a succession of apothecaries; from then on, the owner was styled "druggist"; by the early nineteenth century he called himself a "dispensing chemist." There is abundant evidence from the provinces of a sophisticated, shop-based trade in medicines from the seventeenth century, initially chiefly in the hands of apothecaries, but increasingly being taken over, commonly well before 1780, by mere druggists. John Beatson, for example, was operating as a druggist in Rotherham in 1751, and Wyley in Coventry just a few years later. Similarly, in Chester, a pharmacy had existed since the Restoration. It was traditionally manned by apothecaries—John Goulbourne, John Sudlow, Francis Touchet, and others—from 1722 it was occupied by Peter Ellames, who styled himself "apothecary and druggist," and his sons, in turn, simply called themselves "druggists," apparently preferring retail trade to medical care. We have no reason to suppose that these latter men were any less skilled in the drug business than their predecessors.[34]

The London evidence, as might be expected, reveals an impressively early and powerful presence of shopkeeping druggists operating independently of any medical care. The business of manufacturing chemicals for medicinal and other uses had been strong since the Restoration at least, and in the metropolis, people calling themselves "druggists" rather than "apothecaries" were commanding large slices of the wholesale and retail trade long before the 1780s. Indeed, as early as the 1740s, a spokesman for the Apothecaries Company was bitterly complaining that there were already over a hundred chemists and druggists in town, of whom only twenty were "regular."[35] The first figure may not have been an exaggeration. For while the population of druggists in Georgian London has never been properly measured, a list casually compiled fifty years ago totals 92 chemist's firms and 52 chemist and druggist businesses in operation at some time during the century, and by no means predominantly near the end.[36]

Not untypical of these was the establishment of John Toovey, druggist and chemist at the Black Lion in the Strand, whose mid-eighteenth-century advertisements stated that he made up "all Sorts of Chemical and Galenical Medicines, . . . the very best French and English Hungary Waters, Lavender and Mineral Waters, Daffy's and Stoughton's Elixir, etc. Wholesale and Retail. . . . Physicians Prescriptions made. . . . Chests of Medicines for Gentlemen and Exportation."[37] In London as in the provinces, shops founded by apothecaries tended to be taken over during the course of the century by proprietors simply styling themselves "druggists and chemists," which must sometimes have signalled the fact that they had not undergone a medical apprenticeship.[38] Thus the Plough Court pharmacy was run from 1715 by Silvanus Bevan, who styled himself "apothecary," but from 1765, it came under the management of Timothy Bevan, who called his premises "Druggists and Chemists."[39] Indeed, chemists and druggists clearly played a major role in the enterprise of medicine from the latter half of the seventeenth century. The attempt of the apothecaries from the 1790s, particularly through the General Pharmaceutical Association of Great Britain, founded in 1794, to persuade Parliament to ban unqualified dispensing by druggists is often taken as marking the late and sudden rise of such chemists. Against this, however, it must be remembered that the apothecaries had already waged—and lost—an almost identical campaign against the druggists as early as the 1740s.[40]

Many of the early druggists had businesses big by any standards. In 1710, Anthony Kingsley, a wholesale druggist in Newgate Street, London, went into partnership with his apprentice Edward Pincke and Anselm Beaumont. Between them, they put up capital totalling no less than £8,000.[41] Numerous other family firms or partnerships in pharmaceutical manufacture prospered right through the eighteenth century. Among them were the Bevans' pharmacy at Plough

Court, which eventually became Allen and Hanbury's; Richard Battley's at St. Paul's Churchyard, ultimately taken over by Thomas Keating of flea-powder fame; Thomas Fynmore's pharmacy in Aldersgate Street; Samuel Towers's premises in Oxford Road; and Thomas Bratton's in Castle Street. All these businesses had continuous histories stretching forward into the twentieth century.[42]

Some grew to an impressive size. William Jones's firm provides a good instance.[43] Jones first practiced as a druggist in Little Russell Street, in 1757 moving, rather appropriately, to premises in Great Russell Street as his operation expanded. He secured the plum contract for supplying antimony and cream of tartar to Dr. Robert James, patentee of Dr. James' Fever Powders (his order book for 1772 notes "the usual 500lb of antimony" for James). Jones personally undertook twice-yearly rides around the country angling for orders, and exploited the business potential of the newly-founded county hospitals by securing contracts to supply the infirmaries at Chester, Hereford, Salisbury, and Stafford. Over a period of many years he sold drugs valued at nearly £200 per annum to the Westminster Hospital. Jones traded wholesale to apothecaries and surgeons all over the Midlands and the West Country, and also developed a giant export trade, particularly with the West Indies, Canada, Gibraltar, and the East India Company, as well as with France. So successful was he, that he turned part-time banker, bill-broker, and money-lender—he loaned money to John Hunter—handled India Bonds for his customers, and dealt in lottery tickets and fire insurance. Yet he did not neglect his shop and retail business: his accounts show him selling ten-penny quantities of senna, laudanum, and sassafras to individual customers. When John Hunter urged Edward Jenner to set up "Jenner's Tartar Emetic" as a nostrum, he thought Jones would market it best.

A similar story could be told for the pharmacy which Silvanus Bevan took over from Salem Osgood at Plough Court in 1715.[44] The business was passed down to his brother Timothy in 1765, then to his sons, Timothy II and Silvanus II, and subsequently on to Joseph Gurney Bevan, who ran it until 1794, when it was acquired, briefly, by Samuel Mildred. Mildred in turn went into partnership with William Allen, who finally took on Luke Howard as his partner. The business was clearly stable and prosperous.

Through the century, the bulk of the Plough Court trade lay in drug manufacture and distribution, though a retail department was retained, and Silvanus Bevan practiced physick from the shop. The business, in Quaker hands, had a reputation for high standards of purity and fair dealing: the drugs, it was explained, were genuine rather than cheap. Unfortunately—and this is true of much written on early pharmaceutical concerns—the day-to-day business history of the pharmacy from the Bevans to Allen and Howard is little known. Two full-length books have been written about Plough Court and its proprietors, but these volumes, echoing all the traditional snobberies, dwell upon the high-mindedness of the Bevans, of Allen and Howard: their practical philanthropy, their part in crusading against the slave trade, their contributions to the sciences of chemistry, mineralogy, meteorology, and geology. But they say almost nothing about the networks of buying and selling pharmaceuticals, the economy connecting wholesale chemical suppliers and the doctors and medical institutions which purchased their wares, or indeed about the capital, investment, and profit involved.[45] Though the drugs trade became the linchpin—even the epitome—of the practice of medicine, we have no structured analysis of it, nor any clear idea of its financial dimensions.

In the rest of this paper, we aim to make a preliminary contribution to this basic research task by discussing the business records of one of the largest—though almost wholly neglected—eighteenth-century pharmaceutical manufacturers, Thomas Corbyn, the bulk of which have recently been acquired by, and are available at, the Wellcome Institute for the History of Medicine.[46]

A Quaker, born in Worcestershire in 1711, Thomas Corbyn was apprenticed in 1728 to Joseph Clutton, a London apothecary, also from Worcestershire.[47] Clutton had real medical interests, though it is not known to what extent it was medicine or the pharmacy trade which earned him his living. On Clutton's death in 1743, Thomas Corbyn got his freedom from the Society of Apothecaries, and jointly ran the business with Clutton's widow, a development which suggests that its pharmaceutical side was already well established. Indeed, shortly before Clutton's death, and presumably anticipating it, Corbyn began to send out batches of letters over his own name to correspondents, chiefly abroad, offering to supply them with compound medicines, etc.[48]

In 1747, Corbyn entered into a partnership with Clutton's son, Morris, himself freed from the Apothecaries Company in that year. Each put up nearly £2,000 in capital.[49] Morris Clutton died, however, just seven years later, and Corbyn, having successfully raised thousands of pounds in capital to buy out Clutton's heirs, took over the business single-handed.[50] This arrangement did not prove permanent, and Corbyn traded with a succession of partners for the last thirty years of his life. In 1762, for instance, he entered into an agreement with John Brown and Nicholas Marshall. Marshall evidently proved to be somewhat dubious in his business affairs, and for some time after his death in 1776 much of Corbyn's correspondence was preoccupied with sorting out the mess he left behind. By 1781, Thomas Corbyn's partners were his son John, John Brown, John Beaumont, and George Stacy; in 1787, Brown was replaced by Josiah Messer; in 1795, Beaumont dropped out; and so forth. By the later part of the nineteenth century, the enterprise was known as "Corbyn and Stacey."[51]

What was the nature of the business? Joseph Clutton seems to have combined operating as a chymist with a certain interest in medicine itself. Amongst other things, he published *A short and certain method of curing continuous fevers*.[52] There is no sign, however, that either Thomas Corbyn or Morris Clutton, though freemen of the Apothecaries Company, spent any time caring for the sick. In legal documents, Corbyn was habitually referred to as a "chymist" or "druggist," rather than "apothecary" (though he occasionally styled himself a "wholesale apothecary"). To one correspondent he wrote, "the drug trade is my proper business," noting quite candidly that "it will pay better than any other merchandize."[53]

Corbyn's business lay in the manufacture and sale of drugs, both wholesale and retail, though the former comprised the heart of the enterprise. Catalogues, stock-lists, warehouse records, and elaborate recipe books reveal that Corbyn's made and vended simple drugs like senna, rhubarb, clove oil, arrow root, and bark; compound medicines and galenicals, such as theriac, tartar emetic, Balsamic Tincture, Hungary Water, Citron Water, and hundreds more; and manufactured, or sold, nostrums like Bateman's Pectoral Drops, Daffy's Elixir, and such toiletries as dentrifice.[54] Joseph Clutton had marketed his own nostrum, "Clutton's Febrifuge," but Corbyn—who had a reputation as a stern, no-nonsense Quaker—never attached his own name to proprietary medicines, and nostrum-mongering amounted to only a sliver of the business. Indeed, what is impressive is the dedicated care Corbyn's put into the manufacture of high-quality drugs, made to the College Pharmacopoeia standards.

The Company possessed massive recipe books, listing the ingredients and proportions for several hundred different preparations, together with lengthy and precise instructions for pounding, blending, distillation, and so forth. Many of the recipes have notes appended in later hands, which record experiments for improving manufacturing techniques, occasional failures, recommendations for alternative methods, tips for removing impurities or eradicating unpleasant coloration, and so forth.[55] Most recipes contain itemized costing details, and recommended wholesale prices for the finished product. Thus, for instance, Edinburgh Theriac could be made up by two different processes, one costing 30s. per pound, the other 23s.[56] Corbyn's letters to his customers reveal that he relied on consistent quality, not cheapness or innovation. In 1750 he wrote to John and Esther White in America,[57]

The simple drugs are ye best of their kind, and ye compositions not only true, but curiously prepared, and charg'd reasonable according to ye present market prices. . . . Perhaps some will say ye compositions are too dear, thou must insist on their goodness. I know there are a great many very bad and adulterated medicines sent to America, which are sold cheap but have much larger proffitt than those who are conscientious in preparing them true according to ye London dispensatory.

This approach evidently paid off well, for Corbyn's business grew rapidly but lastingly. In 1750 he could write to Cadwallader Evans, "we confine ourselves pretty much to the Drug Trade, being considerably increas'd."[58]

Corbyn traded from premises at 300 Holborn (later, further premises were taken at Poultry in the City). He had a separate laboratory, and a vast warehouse in Cold Bath Fields. His warehouse stock book or inventory, dated December 1761, runs to 2,500 different items of materia medica, which were stored in extraordinarily large quantities—he held 276 pounds of senna and 806 of magnesia alba for example.[59] Corbyn also made up his drugs in impressively large batches: the recipes not infrequently require ingredients by the hundred-weight. Thus, that for bark extract begins with instructions to digest 150 pounds of bark with 90 gallons of spirit; similarly, the recipe books envisage making up tartar emetic to 365 pounds. Corbyn's records show that compound medicines were manufactured in batches whose cost price often ran to £50 or more, and whose wholesale value to Corbyn may have been twice that amount.[60]

Surviving wage books likewise confirm the scale of the concern. The evidence here is fragmentary, but it appears that the firm had in the region of ten employees at any one time in the 1760s, some of whom were presumably apprentices, and others journeymen.[61] The pricings in the recipe books often include a substantial sum under "labour," ten shillings for instance. Drug manufacture was undoubtedly labor-intensive, involving as it did a long series of stages from bidding at auctions held at Garraway's Coffee House and elsewhere for sacks of raw supplies straight off the East India vessels, through to the final dispatch of orders in neatly-labelled glass bottles, sent across the world, properly packed, insured, and addressed. One set of instructions for preparing ambergris for sale notes that 73 pounds were purchased from John Wheeler; it was refined in "40 operations," requiring 20 bushels of coal and one man's time for seven weeks (the cost of the labor came to £3.6s.8d.).[62]

Other scraps of evidence suggest that Corbyn's was a very busy enterprise. A surviving page of a day book, listing a day's business and takings—interestingly it is for Christmas Day 1761, or "25.12." as Corbyn, staunch Quaker, insisted on calling it—seems to indicate that about 120 separate items were made up that day, comprising about a dozen orders.[63]

The real proof of the scale and success of the enterprise is contained in some fragmentary accounts for the partnership, and by extensive, though often tantalizing, legal bonds, records of loans, borrowings, and partnership agreements. These indicate the magnitude of capital involved. In the 1750s, Thomas Corbyn borrowed upwards of £7,460 from private individuals, mainly Quakers. Joseph Scott alone loaned him £2,400 and he obtained £600 from his

fellow chemist, Timothy Bevan.[64] There is not the slightest indication that the firm suffered any financial crisis; rather, it seems that
Corbyn borrowed so heavily in order to underwrite and expand his
export trade. The fact that cautious Quakers were willing to vest
their money in him indicates their confidence in the enterprise.
Indeed, none of the firm's records, through well into the nineteenth
century, gives the slightest hint of any real financial upsets conse-
quent upon over-expansion, bad management, or even external
events.

When Morris Clutton and Thomas Corbyn went into partnership
in 1747, the business seems to have been worth about £4,000.[65]
Subsequent documents suggest that by the 1780s it was worth
around £20,000. For one year only, 1770, do we have a clear profit-
and-loss account. This shows that the total stock at the beginning
of the year amounted to £5,545. Each month, fresh stock to the
value of between £700 and £1,400 was purchased. Overall, the firm
laid out £9,452 on raw materials in that year (unfortunately, we
have hardly any information as to how Corbyn obtained his basic
supplies). The firm incurred something like £2,000 of further expenses (presumably wages, leases, rates, taxes, and the like). Sales
fluctuated from month to month, from a low of £493 in December
to a peak of £2,150 in February; total sales amounted to £13,966.
As a result, Corbyn's operated with a balance of just over £2,114
clear profit on the year, a tidy sum for frugal Quakers, even when
split between four partners.[66]

Moreover, like all businessmen then, Corbyn spread his irons
among several fires. He often shipped consignments of other merchandise alongside his medicaments to his overseas agents and customers—gloves, shoes, or haberdashery.[67] And above all, he inevit-
ably acted as a bill-broker, discounter, and *de facto* banker, especially
to his overseas clients. In fact, a high proportion of the surviving
business records comprise legal or quasi-legal records of financial
transactions. It is hard to say whether Corbyn and his partners
voluntarily undertook these dealings: some must have unavoidably
arisen out of the necessity of collecting debts from deceased clients'
estates, or from clients who defaulted or could pay only through the
most Byzantine financial manipulations. Certainly, bad debts were
a constant nightmare. All the same, Corbyn was never less than
strict in his financial dealings—the business letters show him to have
been a veritable money-making machine—and it is most unlikely
that he undertook these general financial services without advantage
to himself.[68]

How much, then, was the business actually worth? We lack the
continued runs of figures with which we could answer this question.
But a balance sheet of the partnership between Corbyn and Morris
Clutton between 1746 and 1754, the year Clutton died, gives some
indication of its early scale. Between them, they invested nearly

£4,000 in the partnership. By the time Clutton died, the concern seems to have been worth close to £14,000. In other words the business had expanded by about 350% within eight years. How did this break down? In 1754, some £3,293 was tied up in stock. A further £1,520 was accounted for as "good debts" in what was known as the "Town Apothecaries Ledger," which recorded purchases made by London dispensing apothecaries. Then, £5,318, which obviously formed the bulk of Corbyn and Clutton's domestic wholesale trade, was listed in the "Country Ledger." A further £105 was in their "Patients' Ledger," presumably the retail business. And another £1,978 came from good debts in their "Foreign Ledger." Unfortunately it is not possible to make a breakdown of the changing fortunes of the business from year to year.[69]

But every indication is that it grew steadily. Drafts of letters show that Corbyn's agents overseas routinely owed him sums which ran into several hundreds of pounds, and occasionally into four figures. An inventory of the estate of one of the partners, John Beaumont, taken in 1794, shows he was worth a very respectable £23,000, though a proportion of this certainly derived from lands he owned.[70]

With whom did Corbyn trade? Mention of a "Patient's Account" proves that he had a retail trade, probably both over the counter and by post. This was marginal to the business's overall profits, although its existence helps underline the fact that it would be anachronistic to posit any rigid division between wholesale and retail druggists for this period. Our records of the remainder of Corbyn's domestic trade are slight. There is no surviving correspondence for this branch of the business, and we must rely upon the scanty evidence of a few sales ledgers. These demonstrate that Corbyn's attracted a certain amount of custom from the most fashionable metropolitan practitioners, including John Ranby, Messenger Monsey, William Bromfield, and John Fothergill. (Fothergill, another Quaker, was also a personal friend).[71] More lucratively the business also received a number of regular, substantial orders annually. Several of these came from such London Hospitals as St. George's, Guy's, and St. Thomas's. In 1764, for example, St. George's bought £127 of goods from Corbyn's. Accounts running into hundreds of pounds were also formed with London apothecaries, mainly, one presumes, those who did a handsome trade by dispensing for fashionable physicians. Corbyn's also got business from other London manufacturing chemists, including Sylvanus and Timothy Bevan (who seem to have bought goods worth about £30 a year), and Dalmohoy (who in 1762 spent £30 with Corbyn).[72]

But most of the orders—we are talking of hundreds—came from provincials, many of whom are identifiable as country surgeons and apothecaries. Typically, a sum of between £5 and £30 changed hands annually: Daniel Sutton the inoculator, for example, did business reaching £7.10s. in 1779. Some provincials laid out far more. Thus

John Bogle, the Glasgow surgeon, bought goods worth £217 in 1764. Presumably many of these country customers were small-town druggists or owners of general stores. Since some are listed with "& Co.," it is reasonable to suppose that some were middlemen, shippers, merchants, and smaller wholesalers.[73] It is not known precisely how Corbyn attracted provincial custom. He certainly travelled on business outside London, however, and he, his partners, or their agents may well have ridden around the country, acting the part of early commercial travellers. The account books list "presents" of drugs: if these were not charitable gifts, they may have been free promotional samples.[74] What is clear beyond doubt is that no small part of Corbyn's trade was stimulated and sustained by the Quaker grapevine.

Corbyn's domestic trade was substantial, although for want of documentation it remains obscure. Thanks to the survival of letterbooks, we know more about his exports, and all the signs are that export came to constitute the key growth sector in his business, and to provide the bulk of the profit. Joseph Clutton may or may not have exported drugs on any scale. Copies of the relevant letters, beginning a brand-new letter-book, reveal beyond doubt, however, that in the months before Clutton's death the young Thomas launched a massive export drive. He made contact with a couple of dozen people abroad, a few in continental countries such as Portugal, but principally in the Americas, ranging from Nova Scotia and New England southwards to Jamaica and Antigua. These were surgeons, physicians, dealers, and general agents. Some were personally known to him; most were not. Almost all were Quakers.[75]

Corbyn's technique was to dispatch, unasked, a chestful of drugs, probably about £50 worth. He would suggest to the recipients that they do business on a sale-or-return basis, and asked them to distribute the drugs, parcelled up into appropriate quantities, to local medical practitioners and also to planters and other substantial personages (he considerately enclosed a supply of small bottles and vials for the purpose). Corbyn specified a minimum wholesale price, below which he was, as a rule, unwilling to go, as well as an "advanced" price. Sometimes he would also send lists of potential purchasers he wished his agents to contact, occasionally accompanied by a word of diplomatic advice: he recommended that Isaac Greenleaf, for example, make contact with William Goldsborough of Choptank, Maryland, but warned, "act with caution, he's Jno. Hanbury's friend." The overriding aim was to encourage his contacts to extend outlets. As he instructed Greenleaf, in New York,[76]

Endeavour to settle a Correspondence with proper Merchants for disposal of drugs per commission, at the four following places, viz., Williamsburg, Virginia; Anapolis, Maryland; New York, Newport, Rode Island.

To this end, Corbyn enclosed for Greenleaf the draft of a letter he wanted despatched to such people. It began:[77]

I have herewith sent a small chest, a sortment of those articles in most common use, which are choice good of their kind, and to judges will recommend their selves. My design is to supply yee with a proper stock and sortment that thou may serve the doctors and planters, especially those who do not commonly send their orders directly to London.

Corbyn instructed his agents that the articles might be split up into proper saleable quantities, stating that he was including both items of materia medica and also compounds like Stoughton's Elixir, and Bateman's Pectoral Drops.

Agents were obviously free to make what profit they could. They were, however, to send closely-itemized sales details to Corbyn— ever attentive to the minutiae of the trade—and to arrange for bills which could be drawn upon London bankers. They were given twelve months' credit: Corbyn knew that he could not expect payment sooner, but would chivvy if it were delayed much longer. He was constantly seeking enlightenment from his informants about possible new markets. Whence did the locals already get their drugs, from London or elsewhere? How did Corbyn's prices compare? What sort of items were in ready supply, or in demand? Corbyn allowed his agents some discretion, but was not slow to chide them when they ignored his instructions, or indeed seemed likely to become tardy payers.[78]

Corbyn's bold initiative paid excellent dividends. One surviving letter book contains copies of some 550 business letters, mainly from Corbyn himself to his outlets on the other side of the Atlantic in the period from 1742–55.[79] They chronicle the immense difficulties of dealing over several thousand miles: endless losses, breakages, spoilage, market vagaries, bad debtors, and so on. But they also demonstrate that these were triumphantly overcome by a man of resolution and an iron business temper. Most of Corbyn's outlets clearly had no difficulty in disposing of drug consignments, and they seem to have been happy to deal with him. Letter after letter to such dealers as John Pleasants of Virginia, George Robins of Maryland, Samuel Sansom, Thomas Lightfoot, Israel Pemberton, Esther White, Edward Pennington, and Christopher Marshall (a cousin of John Bartram the naturalist), all of Pennsylvania, Daniel Lathrop of Norwich, Connecticut, John Easton and Jabez Bowen of Newport, Rhode Island, Elijah Collins of Boston, Samuel Bowne, and Peter Renaudot of New York, Robert James of Antigua, Magee of Nova Scotia, Cadwallader Evans of Jamaica, and Dr. Joseph Gamble of Bridgetown, Barbados, testify to sound business relations, giving details of further batches being made up, packed in chests or casks, insured, and sent down to Bristol to await ship.

The business went from strength to strength. Some agents traded very heavily. As early as 1762, John Hunt owed Corbyn £5,640.[80] A letter-book from the early nineteenth century shows a similar trade pattern, but with even larger quantities. One Canadian agent,

William Philipps of Halifax, Nova Scotia, was routinely sending orders, of which some were for colonial hospitals, totalling thousands of pounds. Dealings with Australia begin to appear.[81] And there is evidence of overseas customers contacting the firm on their own initiative. Thus, a letter dated 4 November 1828, from one Peter Stryker, of Somerville, New Jersey.[82]

Gentlemen,

> Having it in contemplation in consequence of the increasing population of our village and its vicinity, to set up an apothecary's shop in the village of Somerville in which I reside—have thought it expedient to embrace the opportunity afforded by my friend A. Stoadart Esq. of the City of London and on his recommendation to send you this small medical order, which I hope will be executed on a credit sufficient for me to make a remittance in season to meet your expectations.

Stryker went on to ask the prices of various articles, and attached an order running to no fewer than 130 items, beginning with seven pounds of opium and including most of the standard materia medica, as well as bottles, stoppers, and so forth.

Corbyn and Partners were one of the number—probably a few dozen—of large London firms of druggists which emerged during the eighteenth century. In many cases, no records exist. However, sufficient papers survive from Corbyn's, the Plough Court pharmacy, Jones's, and a few others, to make serious research on the eighteenth-century origins of the pharmaceutical industry a viable, as well as a fascinating, project. For now, we should like to suggest a few interim conclusions.

First, the Quaker connection was of quite paramount importance to Corbyn's rise to prominence. His correspondence proves that it was the moral and business codes of the Quaker International which made long-distance, indeed trans-Atlantic, trade in drugs a viable enterprise.[83] The young Corbyn was able, with confidence, to send large and expensive consignments of drugs to people who had never heard of him, and they, in turn, felt able to buy from him with confidence, and all essentially because they had a special relation with those people they habitually addressed as "Loving Friend." They felt trust in their business probity, and anyway knew that in the case of default, the Quaker community would not be slow to put on the screws. Such credit and confidence were absolutely indispensable to the rapid expansion of long-distance trade.

Second, it would be likewise difficult to exaggerate the significance of overseas markets—Corbyn in North America, Jones with the East India Company—for the expansion of the pharmaceutical trade. Alfred Crosby has suggested that eighteenth- and nineteenth-century British imperialism could hardly have been so successful without the drugs which rendered unhealthy tropical environments rather less crowded with white man's graves, or indeed black slaves' graves, than they might have been.[84] Richard Sheridan has recently shown how extensive were the medical arrangements necessary to keep the plantations going. Because the colonies and even the independent United States were slow to develop their own drugs industries, the pickings available for London firms prepared to take risks, time, trouble, and expense, were rich indeed.[85]

Third, business records like Corbyn's indicate that we need to revise our stereotypes of the druggists. Doubtless, some were as the apothecaries represented them: vermin who scuttled in to occupy the shops vacated by the apothecaries themselves; ignorant hucksters out to make a fast buck; threats to health because of their medical ignorance, their passion for committing adulteration. Yet some druggists, at least, and we may never know how many, were not like this at all: they were neither ignorant, nor parasitical, nor dangerous. It was certainly not the case that the druggists' trade attracted only lowly, ill-lettered men who had failed to obtain the training which would have qualified them as apothecaries. A scrupulous man such as Corbyn could easily have chosen to practice medicine as an apothecary. Instead, he preferred to manufacture drugs, because that line of trade interested him more, or, most probably, because he realized that the drugs trade was a far more lucrative business. The Bromfield medical dynasty may give another illuminating instance. The eldest son of the first Thomas Bromfield chose to become a druggist; the Bromfield who became a physician was a third son, by a later marriage. As Burnby has remarked, the snobbery which assumes that it was *infra dig.* to be a druggist may be ours more than theirs.[86]

Maybe the "adulteration" slur also requires re-examination. Corbyn was a highly skilled manufacturing chemist and a shrewd business man. He knew his trading reputation hinged upon reliable, high quality products. "I could make 100% profit by adulteration," he once boasted.[87] Such a profit-conscious man knew that adulteration would prove to be a mistake in the long run. Purity and consistency meant more to his success than innovation, science, or mere novelty. One might even reverse the arrow of accusation, and hypothesize that the large manufacturing chemists supplied relatively pure drugs; whereas it was the small-town apothecary, faced with treating the sick poor who could not pay their bills, with the necessity of dispensing a bewildering variety of medicines, and with direct requests for cordials and the like, who might well be tempted to adulterate.

Finally, after too much academic neglect and condescension, it is surely time to acknowledge the key importance of the druggists' emergence to the whole organization, structure, and enterprise of medicine. It is surely beyond dispute that, for better or worse, medical practice came to depend ever more heavily upon the trade in medicines, from the rich hypochondriacal patient with his annual apothecaries' bill of several hundred pounds, down to the dispensary

itself with its free drugs for the poor. We too rarely remember, however, that none of this could have taken place if all grades of clinical
practitioners, hospitals, dispensaries (one might add, ships and ar-
mies), and, not least, the self-medicating individuals themselves,
had not had ready access to reliable supplies of a gamut of medicaments. The making and marketing of drugs provided the commodity upon which the modern business of medicine was founded.

Notes and References

The authors would like to thank Richard Palmer of the Wellcome Institute
for his great help in using the Wellcome Corbyn papers.

1. See P. Wright, 'The radical sociology of medicine,' *Social Studies of
   Science*, 1980, 10: 103-20; *idem* and A. Treacher (eds.), *The problem
   of medical knowledge*, Edinburgh University Press, 1982, introduction.
2. See, for example, S. W. F. Holloway, 'The Apothecaries' act 1815. Part
   1: the origins of the Act,' *Medical History*, 1966; 10: 107-29; 'Part 2:
   the consequences of the Act,' ibid., pp. 221-36; *idem*, 'The orthodox
   fringe: the origins of the Pharmaceutical Society of Great Britain,' in
   W. F. Bynum and Roy Porter (eds.), *Medical fringe and medical orthodoxy, 1750-1850*, London, Croom Helm, 1986, pp. 129-57; Ivan Waddington, *The medical profession in the Industrial Revolution*, Dublin,
   Gill and Macmillan, 1984.
3. J. Raach, *A directory of English country physicians 1603-1643*, London,
   Dawson's, 1962; M. Pelling and C. Webster, 'Medical practitioners', in
   C. Webster (ed.), *Health, medicine and mortality in the sixteenth century*, Cambridge University Press, 1979, pp. 165-235; M. Pelling, 'Appearance and reality: barber-surgeons, the body and disease,' in L. Beier
   and R. Finlay (eds.), *London, 1500-1700: the making of the metropolis*,
   London, Longman, 1986, pp. 82-112; *idem*, 'Healing the sick poor:
   social policy and disability in Norwich 1550-1640,' *Medical History*,
   1985, 29: 115-37.
4. J. G. L. Burnby, *A study of the English apothecary from 1660 to 1760*.
   Medical History Supplement 3, London, Wellcome Institute, 1983; G.
   Holmes, *Augustan England: professions, state and society 1680-1730*,
   London, Wellcome Institute, 1983; G. Holmes, *Augustan England:
   professions, state and society 1680-1730*, London, George Allen & Un-
   win, 1982; Joan Lane, 'The medical practitioners of provincial England
   in 1783,' *Medical History* 1984, 28: 353-71; *idem*, 'The provincial practitioner and his services to the poor,' *Bulletin of the Society for the
   Social History of Medicine*, 1981, 28: 10-14; Irvine Loudon, 'The nature
   of provincial medical practice in eighteenth-century England,' *Medical
   History*, 1985, 29: 1-32.
5. M. J. Peterson, *The medical profession in mid-Victorian London*, Berkeley and Los Angeles, University of California Press, 1978.
6. Irvine Loudon, 'A doctor's cash-book: the economy of general practice
   in the 1830s,' *Medical History*, 1983, 27: 249-68; E. M. Sigsworth and
   P. Swan, 'An eighteenth-century surgeon and apothecary: William Elm-
   hirst (1721-73),' ibid., 1982, 26: 191-8; D'Arcy Power, 'The fees of our

ancestors,' in *Selected writings 1877–1930*, Oxford University Press, 1931, pp. 95–102.

7. See Sir G. Clark, *A history of the Royal College of Physicians of London*, 3 vols., Oxford University Press, 1964–72; Sir Zachary Cope, *The history of the Royal College of Surgeons of England*, London, Anthony Blond, 1959; C. Wall, *A history of the Worshipful Society of Apothecaries of London*, vol. 1, *1617–1815*, London, Oxford University Press, 1963; H. J. Cook, *The decline of the old medical regime in Stuart London*, Ithaca, Cornell University Press, 1986.

8. J. Bell and T. Redwood, *Historical sketch of the progress of pharmacy in Great Britain*, London, The Pharmaceutical Society of Great Britain, 1880, p. 30.

9. Ibid.

10. See A. Scull, 'A Victorian alienist: John Conolly FRCP DCL (1794–1866),' in W. F. Bynum, Roy Porter, and Michael Shepherd (eds.), *The anatomy of madness*, 2 vols., London, Tavistock, 1985, vol. 1, pp. 103–51.

11. Unfortunately, the history of pharmacy has been little studied. For broad surveys see L. Matthews, *History of pharmacy in Britain*, Edinburgh and London, E. & S. Livingston, 1962; J. Grier, *A history of pharmacy*, London, The Pharmaceutical Press, 1937; F. N. L. Poynter (ed.), *The evolution of pharmacy in Britain*, London, Pitman, 1965; J. K. Crellin, 'Pharmaceutical history and its sources in the Wellcome Collections. 1: The growth of professionalism in nineteenth-century British pharmacy,' *Medical History*, 1967, 11: 215–27; Bell and Redwood, op. cit., note 8 above. Some of the hidden assumptions in much of this literature are exposed in Holloway, 'The orthodox fringe,' op. cit. note 2 above.

12. R. S. Roberts, 'The early history of the import of drugs into Britain,' in Poynter (ed.), op. cit., note 11 above, pp. 165–86.

13. C. Webster, *The great instauration. Science, medicine and reform 1626–1660*. London, Duckworth, 1975; A. Debus, *The English Paracelsians*, London, Oldbourne, 1965; O. Hannaway, *The chemists and the word*, Baltimore, Johns Hopkins University Press, 1975; M. B. Hall, 'Apothecaries and chemists in the seventeenth century,' *Pharmaceutical Journal*, 28 Oct. 1967, pp. 433–6.

14. See Cook, op. cit., note 7 above, ch. 4; Bell and Redwood, op. cit., note 8 above, p. 13. The idea of a chemical laboratory was first mooted in 1641 by Edward Cooke, Master of the Society.

15. Roy Porter, 'The patient in the eighteenth century,' in A. Wear (ed.), *The history of medicine in society*, Cambridge University Press, (forthcoming).

16. For a classic exposition see B. Mandeville, *A treatise of the hypochondriack and hysterick diseases*, London, J. Tonson, 1730.

17. C. A. Moore, 'The English malady,' in *Backgrounds of English literature, 1700–1760*, Minneapolis, University of Minnesota Press, 1953; Roy Porter, 'The rage of party: A Glorious Revolution in English psychiatry?,' *Medical History*, 1983, 29: 35–50.

18. See Cook, op. cit., note 7 above, ch. 6; Bell and Redwood, op. cit., note 8 above, p. 15; Irvine Loudon, 'The origins and growth of the dispensary movement in England,' *Bulletin of the History of Medicine*, 1981, 55: 322–42; L. G. Matthews, 'The Aldersgate Dispensary and the Alders-

gate Medical School,' *Pharmaceutical Historian*, 1983, 13: 7–8. Hal Cook has obligingly emphasized to us that many of the developments which we here discuss in respect of the end of the seventeenth century and beginning of the eighteenth had a longer history; we are entirely in agreement with this view.

19. See W. F. Bynum and Roy Porter (eds.), *Medical fringe and medical orthodoxy, 1750–1850*, London, Croom Helm, 1986; Roy Porter, 'Before the fringe: quack medicine in Georgian England,' *History Today*, October 1986, pp. 16–22; and *idem, Health for sale: quack medicine in England*, Manchester University Press, 1989.

20. See C. J. S. Thompson, *The mystery and art of the apothecary*, London, John Lane, 1929, p. 199. See also the discussion in Bell and Redwood, op. cit., note 8 above, pp. 18ff.

21. Holmes, op. cit., note 4 above, p. 186. The College of Physicians actually brought the case.

22. See the discussion in Holloway, 'The orthodox fringe,' op. cit., note 2 above.

23. E.g., F. F. Cartwright, *A social history of medicine*, London, Longman, 1977, pp. 52–3.

24. See Bell and Redwood, op. cit., note 8 above, p. 27; Thompson, op. cit., note 20 above, pp. 194ff; on this subject, Burnby, op. cit., note 4 above, is a fundamental work of research and reinterpretation.

25. Loudon, op. cit., note 4 above.

26. See *idem*, 'The Vile Race of Quacks with which this Country is Infested,' in Bynum and Porter (eds.), op cit., note 19 above, pp. 106–28; on Broderip, p. 107.

27. On this Holmes, op. cit., note 4 above, pp. 229ff. is valuable.

28. See Loudon, op. cit., note 26 above.

29. Bell and Redwood, op. cit., note 8 above, p. 34; J. M. Good, *The history of medicine, so far as it relates to the profession of the apothecary*, London, Dilly, 1796, p. 148, for "encroachment." Good urged (p. 227) "the entire restoration ... of retail pharmacy to the apothecary" as "just."

30. See the remarks in S. W. F. Holloway, 'The orthodox fringe,' op. cit., note 19 above, pp. 129–57, especially pp. 154–5.

31. See Loudon, op. cit., note 26 above, pp. 108, 109; *idem, Medical care and the general practitioner 1750–1850*, Oxford, Clarendon Press, 1986, pp. 133ff. Valuable suggestions are offered in J. G. L. Burnby, 'Some Flinders family history: connection with pharmacy,' *Australian Journal of Pharmacy*, 1987, 68: 61–6.

32. See the information in Loudon, op. cit., note 26 above, especially pp. 111ff. There is useful corroboration in G. Fletcher and J. I. Harris, 'Pharmacy in Bath during the Regency period,' *Pharmaceutical Historian*, 1970, 5: 2–4; W. J. Robinson, 'Physick in Bolton in 1779,' ibid., 1981, 11: 6–7; W. L. B. Coleman, *The chemists and pharmacists of Norwich and district from c. 1800 to 1975*, Norwich, The Author, 1977; J. Austen, *Historical notes on old Sheffield druggists*, Sheffield, Northend, 1961. For some comments on the use of trade directories, see. J. G. L. Burnby, 'Apprenticeship records,' *Transactions of the British Society for the History of Pharmacy*, 1977, 1: 145–94.

33. For similar information, see *idem*, 'Some Derbyshire apothecaries,' *Pharmaceutical Historian*, 1970, 5: 5–8.

34. For the crucial importance of the shop see J. K. Crellin, 'Pharmacies as general stores in the 19th century,' *Pharmaceutical Historian*, April, 1979, 9: [unpaginated]; Laurence Dopson, 'The state of London chemists' shops in the 18th and early 19th centuries,' *Chemist and Druggist*, Annual Special Issue, 25 June 1955, pp. 718–21; L. G. Matthews, 'The spicers and apothecaries of Norwich,' *Pharmaceutical Journal*, 1967, 198: 5–9.
35. See Bell and Redwood, op. cit., note 8 above, pp. 33, 34.
36. [Anon.] 'Eighteenth-century London chemists,' *Chemist and Druggist*, 1937, 127: 178–9; [anon.], 'Retail pharmacy over one hundred years,' *Pharmaceutical Journal*, 1941, 141: 130–63.
37. Burnby, op. cit., note 4 above, p. 53.
38. Ibid., p. 60.
39. E. C. Cripps, *Plough Court. The story of a notable pharmacy*, London, Allen and Hanbury, 1927; D. Chapman-Huston and E. C. Cripps, *Through a city archway: the story of Allen and Hanbury, 1715–1954*, London, Murray, 1954.
40. Loudon, op. cit., note 26 above, esp. pp. 118ff.; Holloway, op. cit., note 30 above, pp. 130ff.; Bell and Redwood, op. cit., note 8 above, pp. 36ff.; Wall, op. cit., note 7 above, p. 148.
41. Matthews, op. cit., note 11 above, p. 215.
42. Matthews, op. cit., note 11 above, pp. 224ff.; [anon.], 'Pharmaceutical houses of London,' *Chemist and Druggist*, 1953, 575–8. See also J. G. L. Burnby, 'The Towers and the Huskissons,' *Pharmaceutical Journal*, 21 June 1980, pp. 716–18.
43. Extremely valuable for the following details is G. M. Watson, 'Some eighteenth-century trading accounts,' in Poynter, op. cit., note 11 above, pp. 45–78. See also Burnby, op. cit., note 4 above, p. 51.
44. See Cripps, op. cit., note 39 above; Chapman-Huston and Cripps, op. cit., note 39 above.
45. See Cripps, op. cit., note 39 above; Chapman-Huston and Cripps, op. cit., note 39 above. The latter book has some discussion of exports, (pp. 38ff.). These works at least have the merit of demonstrating that mere druggists were not "marginal men." For important confirmation of this point, see P. Weindling, 'Geological controversy and its historiography: the prehistory of the Geological Society of London,' in L. J. Jordanova and R. Porter (eds.), *Images of the earth*, Chalfont St. Giles, British Society for the History of Science, 1979, pp. 215–47.
46. Cited henceforth as "Wellcome Corbyn Papers." The contents are described in a typescript finding list, 'Corbyn and Co., Chemists and Druggists, London.' They form Western MSS 5435–5460. It should be emphasized here that this present article is intended to offer no more than a general outline of Corbyn's activities, based upon preliminary work on these papers and others (e.g., sales catalogues) available at the Library of Pharmaceutical Society of Great Britain. It is hoped to publish further work in the near future, examining particular aspects of Corbyn's business in greater depth, on the basis of more systematic study of these manuscripts.
47. For an extremely valuable introduction to Corbyn, see T. D. Whittet and J. G. L. Burnby, 'The firm of Corbyn and Stacy,' *Pharmaceutical Journal*, 1982, 228: 42–8; and the discussion in Burnby, op. cit., note 4 above, pp. 49–51.

48. Ibid., pp. 49–50.
49. Wellcome Corbyn Papers, 5437.
50. Reconstructed from Wellcome Corbyn Papers, co-partnership agreements, 5438, 5439.
51. See deeds and contracts in Wellcome Corbyn Papers, 5438, 5439, 5453–6, 5459.
52. See Whittet and Burnby, op. cit., note 47 above; Wellcome Corbyn Papers, 5436, item 11.
53. Wellcome Corbyn Papers, 5442, Foreign Letter Book, p. 98, letter to Samuel Browne, 7 June 1748.
54. Wellcome Corbyn Papers, 5451, *Preparationes chymicae et galenicae*, a large folio printed broadside (1747); for Corbyn's inventory, see 5452. See also Roy Porter and Dorothy Porter, *In sickness and in health: the British experience 1650–1850*. London, Fourth Estate, 1988; and Dorothy Porter and Roy Porter, *Patient's progress*, Cambridge, Polity, 1989.
55. Wellcome Corbyn Papers, 5450 (1); 5450 (2) is more-or-less a copy. They run to over 200 pages, and are alphabetically arranged. The annotations date from 1748 to 1841.
56. Wellcome Corbyn Papers, 5450 (1).
57. Wellcome Corbyn Papers, 5442, Foreign Letter Book, p. 76, 7 March 1747.
57. Ibid., p. 132, 18 April 1750.
59. Wellcome Corbyn Papers, 5452 (1–4), Inventory, 1761. The inventory is in four folio volumes, totalling 59 pages. It gives the precise physical location of each item within the warehouse.
60. Wellcome Corbyn Papers, 5450 (1), recipe book.
61. Wellcome Corbyn Papers, 5445.
62. Wellcome Corbyn Papers, 5450 (1). In general, we have only the scantiest information about Corbyn's suppliers of raw materials. His letters to American correspondents give little indication of purchasing from them.
63. Wellcome Corbyn Papers, 5439 (18, 21).
64. Wellcome Corbyn Papers, 5439, 5440 *passim*. Many deeds and bonds are to be found here.
65. Wellcome Corbyn Papers, 5439.
66. Wellcome Corbyn Papers, 5439 (especially item 18), 5437 (1).
67. Wellcome Corbyn Papers, 5442, Foreign Letter Book. The early letters in particular are full of requests for such items. Presumably Corbyn was able to drop these peripheral trades as his business grew more prosperous.
68. Wellcome Corbyn Papers, 5436, 5439, 5460.
69. Wellcome Corbyn Papers, 5451–52.
70. Wellcome Corbyn Papers, 5458.
71. See R. Hingston Fox, *Dr. John Fothergill and his friends*, London, Macmillan, 1919, pp. 264, 282, 339.
72. Wellcome Corbyn Papers, 5437 (1).
73. Wellcome Corbyn Papers, 5439 (12, 18). Corbyn lists the names of his purchasers but not their addresses, making the task of tracking them down for the most part extremely difficult. For the supplying of a provincial general shopkeeper, who sold drugs alongside groceries and other merchandise, see T. S. Willan, *An eighteenth-century shopkeeper: Abraham Dent of Kirkby Stephen*. Manchester University Press, 1970.

74. Wellcome Corbyn Papers, 5439 (5).
75. Wellcome Corbyn Papers, 5442, Foreign Letter Book, provides overwhelming evidence.
76. Wellcome Corbyn Papers, 5442. Foreign Letter Book, p. 36, 15 March 1745. See also C. Spiers, 'The drug supplies of George Washington and other Virginians,' *Pharmaceutical Historian*, 1977, 7, no. 1.
77. Wellcome Corbyn Papers, 5442, Foreign Letter Book, p. 36, 15 March 1745.
78. For good instances wee Wellcome Corbyn Papers, 5442, Foreign Letter Book, correspondence with Christopher Marshall, to be found on pp. 94, 97, 98, 101, 104, 112, 120, 131, 134, 135, 139, 153, 171.
79. Wellcome Corbyn Papers, 5442. Foreign Letter Book. For an invaluable general introduction to contemporary relations between English and American Quakers, see. R. P. Stearns, *Science in the British colonies of America*, Urbana, University of Illinois Press, 1970.
80. Wellcome Corbyn Papers, 5438.
81. Wellcome Corbyn Papers, 5443. Foreign Letter Book.
82. Wellcome Corbyn Papers, 5441 (3/9).
83. A. Raistrick, *Quakers in science and industry*, Newton Abbot, David and Charles, 1968; M. Stiles, 'The Quakers in pharmacy,' in Poynter (ed.), op cit., note 11 above.
84. A. Crosby, *Ecological imperialism: the biological expansion of Europe, 900–1900*, Cambridge University Press, 1986.
85. R. Sheridan, *Doctors and slaves: a medical and demographic history of slavery in the British West Indies, 1680–1834*, Cambridge University Press, 1985.
86. Burnby, op. cit., note 4 above, p. 50.
87. Wellcome Corbyn Papers, 5442, Foreign Letter Book, p. 72, 24 February 1747.

The "Preposterous Provision": The American Society for Pharmacology and Experimental Therapeutics' Ban on Industrial Pharmacologists, 1908–1941

by John Parascandola

READERS familiar with Sinclair Lewis's classic novel *Arrowsmith*, published in 1925, will probably recall the character of Max Gottlieb, the idealistic immunologist who serves as a father figure to the young Martin Arrowsmith. At one point in the narrative, Gottlieb, who has always criticized the commercialism of certain large pharmaceutical firms, is forced for financial reasons to work for one of these companies. When the news of this situation reached the laboratories of great scientists around the world, ". . . sorrowing men wailed 'How could old Max have gone over to that damned pill-peddler?' "[1]

Although this incident is taken from a work of fiction, it reflects a real-life attitude on the part of many academic scientists towards their industrial colleagues in this period and beyond. Perhaps nowhere is this suspicion of scientific work carried out in industrial firms, and specifically in the pharmaceutical industry, better illustrated than in the case of American pharmacology. Industrial pharmacologists were actually banned from membership in the national society for American pharmacologists from its founding in 1908 until 1941.

The birth of modern experimental pharmacology, the science that deals with the investigation of the physiological action of drugs, dates back only to the nineteenth century. The discipline became institutionalized in German medical schools in the second half of

Chief, History of Medicine Division, National Library of Medicine, 8600 Rockville Pike, Bethesda, MD 20894.

the century, replacing the older didactic subject of materia medica, which emphasized the natural origin, composition, means of preparation and administration, and traditional therapeutic uses of drugs.

The Germanic model of experimental pharmacology was brought to the United States by John Jacob Abel, who assumed the chair of materia medica and therapeutics at the University of Michigan in 1891 after six and one-half years of studying biomedical science in Europe. Abel converted the traditional materia medica course at Michigan into a modern course in pharmacology. In 1893, he moved to The Johns Hopkins University, when its medical school opened, to occupy the chair of pharmacology there. He spent the rest of his career at Hopkins, where his laboratory served as the center of American pharmacology for decades.[2]

Other medical schools also began to make the transition from materia medica to pharmacology around the turn of the twentieth century, and by 1908 the American practitioners of this discipline had progressed far enough in their search for a professional identity that they felt the need for an organization of their own. In that year, eighteen men met in Abel's laboratory at Johns Hopkins to found the American Society for Pharmacology and Experimental Therapeutics (ASPET). Most American pharmacologists at the time were based in academia (in medical schools), as is reflected by the fact that eleven of the founders were employed by universities. Five others worked for the Federal government, in the Department of Agriculture or the Hygienic Laboratory of the Public Health Service, and two others were at the Rockefeller Institute for Medical Research.[3]

There were few pharmacologists associated with industry in the United States in 1908, yet the founders of the Society were apparently concerned enough about a potential threat from this quarter to insert the following two clauses into the new organization's constitution:

No one shall be admitted to membership who is in the permanent employ of any drug firm.

Entrance into the permanent employ of a drug firm shall constitute forfeiture of membership.[4]

These steps were taken, in the words of the Society's Council, "in order to avoid every external influence which would be inimical to the scientific interests of pharmacology."[5]

It is not clear who first proposed the ban on industrial pharmacologists. The committee which drafted the constitution consisted of Abel and three of his former associates at Johns Hopkins: Reid Hunt (Chairman), Arthur Loevenhart, and Albert Crawford.[6] Apparently, however, the above clauses were not contained in the first draft of the constitution circulated to the Council. A draft of the

John Jacob Abel, the "Father of American Pharmacology," in his laboratory at The Johns Hopkins University (courtesy of the National Library of Medicine).

document from the files of C.W. Edmunds of the University of
Michigan, a Council member, does not contain these clauses, but
someone has penciled in the words "Employ by firm" in the section
on membership.[7] Another (incomplete) version of the constitution,
also from his files, contains changes in pencil which appear to be
in Abel's hand. These include a new section in the article on membership, banning persons in the permanent employ of drug firms.
It was inserted, however, with the notation "from Loevenhart."[8] Of
course, even if Loevenhart drafted the wording of this clause, the
original suggestion for such a ban could have come from any member of the committee or the Council. It would be ironic if Loevenhart
initiated the idea, because he was later to become one of the most
active leaders in the campaign to eliminate the membership restriction on industrial pharmacologists.

Whoever suggested the ban, it seems to have met with the general
approval of the founders of the Society. There is no evidence in
surviving correspondence and other records that there was any debate over adopting it. On the other hand, these documents do indicate that there was significant discussion about other membership
matters, such as whether or not to admit clinicians who were not
actually engaged in pharmacological research.[9] Apparently no one
saw fit to challenge the prohibition against industrial pharmacologists, and a serious movement to change this rule did not begin for
about another decade. The campaign to eliminate the ban was not
successful until 1941, thirty-three years after the founding of the
Society.

This prohibition against industrial scientists was unique among
American professional scientific societies, so far as I can tell.[10] No
doubt anti-industry bias existed on the part of academic scientists
in other societies, but I do not know of any other case where it was
carried to the extreme of explicitly singling out industry scientists
for exclusion from membership. If we examine three related professional organizations, the American Chemical Society, the American
Physiological Society, and the American Society of Biological Chemists, we find that none of them had such a clause in their constitution.
In fact, all included industrial scientists as members long before the
society of pharmacologists would admit them.

The American Chemical Society, for example, had developed significant ties with industry by the turn of this century. The first
specialized division organized by the Society, in 1907, was the Division of Industrial and Engineering Chemistry, reflecting the large
number of industrial chemists in the Society. Several of the Society's
presidents in the period 1880–1920 were associated with the chemical industry.[11]

The other two societies are particularly relevant from a compar-
ative point of view because of their close relationship with the pharmacology society. Both the American Society of Biological Chemists

and the American Society for Pharmacology and Experimental Therapeutics were offshoots of the American Physiological Society, and the three societies held their meetings together for many years. There was significant overlap in membership between the societies. Abel, for example, was a member of all three.

The American Physiological Society admitted pharmacologist Elijah Houghton of Parke, Davis and Company as a member in 1901. Abel's associate at Johns Hopkins, Thomas Aldrich, was admitted to the physiologists' society in 1895, and did not have to relinquish his membership when he moved to Parke, Davis a few years later. In 1916, Aldrich, still at Parke, Davis, was admitted to membership in the American Society of Biological Chemists.[12]

Pharmacologists who could not be admitted to membership in their own professional society because of the restrictive clause were thus sometimes elected to membership in a sister organization. When Alfred Newton Richards of the University of Pennsylvania wrote to Abel in 1933 to ask him to second the nomination of industrial pharmacologist Hans Molitor of Merck for membership

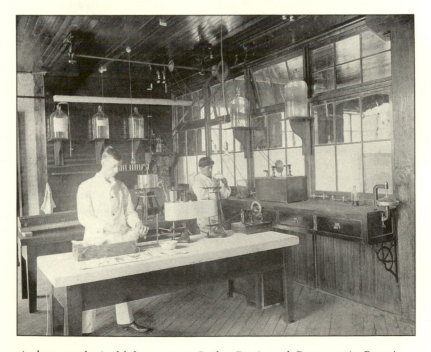

A pharmacological laboratory at Parke, Davis and Company in Detroit around the turn of the twentieth century (courtesy of the Kremers Reference Files, F. B. Power Pharmaceutical Library, University of Wisconsin-Madison).

in the physiological society, for example, he added: "I am not proposing him for membership in the Pharmacological Society because of the rule that people in the permanent employ of commercial firms are ineligible."[13] Evidence that the American Physiological Society may have even stretched their scope to accept pharmacologists who could not be admitted to ASPET because of their industrial employment is provided in the 1939 minutes of the Society. Action was deferred on the membership application of three pharmacologists from industry because "it was thought that the pharmacologists might revise their views regarding commercial pharmacologists," suggesting that the physiologists felt there might be no need to accept these scientists if they could become members of ASPET.[14]

Why then were the pharmacologists so much more concerned than their colleagues about admitting industrial scientists into their national society? What were the external influences "inimical to the scientific interests of pharmacology" that they were trying to avoid? Motivation is usually difficult to establish, and the early leaders of the Society did not leave a completely clear and neat record of justification for their action. The existing evidence allows us, however, to suggest at least some of the concerns which motivated American pharmacologists in this matter.

The industry that most concerned pharmacologists, and the one spelled out in the membership restriction clauses, was the pharmaceutical industry. During the first decade of the twentieth century, when the Society was founded, the American drug industry had a somewhat suspect reputation. Thousands of patent medicines of a dubious nature flooded the market, and patent medicine quackery, brought to public attention by muckraking journalists of the Progressive Era, was one of the factors that led to the passage of a national pure food and drug act in 1906. Although the more legitimate drug firms tried to distance themselves from the patent medicine promoters, they were not completely successful in lifting the cloud of suspicion that hung over the industry as a whole.[15]

Even the so-called "ethical" firms sometimes engaged in practices that pharmacologists considered objectionable. For example, Abel complained that his name had been used without his permission on occasion in drug advertisements or on drug labels. In a 1910 letter to a colleague, he warned: "Even reputable firms will do things that tend to damage men."[16] And five years later he expressed the following skeptical view about the advertising practices of drug manufacturers: "It is well known that the advertisers of drugs and medicines have often failed to confine their statements to actual facts and have yet to get the confidence of our profession."[17]

The traditional opposition of the medical community to patenting medical discoveries, reflected already in the Code of Ethics of the American Medical Association at its founding in 1847, probably influenced the views of many pharmacologists towards research in

Ko Kuei Chen of Eli Lilly and Company, one of the most prominent industrial pharmacologists of the first half of the twentieth century (courtesy of the National Library of Medicine).

commercial firms.[18] Most of the first generation of American pharmacologists were trained as medical doctors, for there were no graduate programs in the subject in the United States. Even those who studied the subject abroad, like Abel, usually received the M.D. degree. Seventeen of the 18 founders of ASPET in 1908, for example, possessed medical degrees. By contrast, only 14 of the 29 founding members of the American Society of Biological Chemists in 1905 had M.D. degrees, and six of them were also founders of ASPET who in most cases considered their profession as pharmacology rather than biochemistry. Certainly only a relatively small proportion of the members of the American Chemical Society had M.D. degrees at the time. On the other hand, the American Physiological Society, which did not ban industry scientists, was also heavily medical in its membership.[19]

Pharmacologists may have been especially sensitive, relative to other scientists, about commercial influences on their work. It was the work of the pharmacologist, rather than that of the chemist or biochemist, that would decide at the experimental level the therapeutic potential and toxicity of a new drug. Academic pharmacologists were concerned that their industrial colleagues were subject to pressures from their employers to emphasize positive results and downplay negative results. Whether or not this was actually the case, it was certainly perceived to be so by many pharmacologists in academia and government. Robert Hatcher of Cornell, for example, expressed these concerns in a 1919 letter:

... nearly all workers in commercial houses deplore the limitations of their work due to the pressure for financially productive results, and to the ne-

cessity of avoiding publications that are inimical to financial interests . . .
you need hardly ask proof that pressure is often put on investigators to
supply desirable results.[20]

Torald Sollmann of Western Reserve University indicated that
the founders of ASPET felt that a pharmacological society was
"obliged to take these peculiar precautions, because otherwise it
would be exposed to peculiar dangers."[21] Similarly, Samuel Meltzer
of the Rockefeller Institute argued that the *Journal of Pharmacology
and Experimental Therapeutics*, founded by Abel in 1909, had to
be more careful about drug advertisements than, for example, a
journal of morphology. He pointed out that many people would
interpret an advertisement in the pharmacological journal as im-
plying authoritative approval of a drug.[22]

Fears were also expressed that industrial pharmacologists might
use the forum provided by the Society's annual meetings to extol
the virtues of the products marketed by their employers. Reid Hunt,
for example, expressed to Abel his concern that "the scientific meetings of the Society might become an opportunity for the reading of
papers on drugs being exploited, or to be exploited, commercially."[23]
The Society was so concerned about this potential problem that
soon after it became a part of the newly-created Federation of American Societies for Experimental Biology in 1912, a motion was
passed to ask that the Federation not transfer any paper to the AS-
PET program without the explicit consent of the Secretary of the
Society. The main purpose of this resolution was to prevent the
appearance on the program of papers of a "commercial nature."[24]

Abel was sensitive, as might be expected, about possible exploitation of the *Journal of Pharmacology and Experimental Therapeutics* for commercial purposes. The first paper from an industrial
laboratory did not appear in the *Journal* until the sixth volume
(1914), and there were few such papers before 1925. On the other
hand, most American pharmaceutical firms were not carrying out
much research that would have been suitable for publication in the
Journal in the first quarter of the century. While there is thus no
clear evidence that Abel actually discriminated against papers from
industrial pharmacologists, he did express the view in 1926 that he
had to be on his guard about criticism in publishing papers from
manufacturing firms. He commented with respect to two of these
papers submitted that year that they "might give the impression of
not being sufficiently impartial from a scientific point of view" and
that "some might get the impression that there is an advertising
element in the papers." His main concern in the case of these two
papers appears to have been the use of the trade names of the drugs
involved. Abel felt that the trade names should be deleted entirely,
or at most mentioned in brackets (following the chemical names)
once or twice near the beginning of the paper, but not in the title
or in any of the tables.[25]

One must also recall that in the early years of the Society, American pharmacology was still struggling to become a legitimate academic discipline. Pharmacologists were trying to escape the role assigned to materia medica, which was often viewed as essentially a handmaiden to therapeutics. Leaders such as John Abel emphasized that pharmacology was a basic biological science, related to but distinct from physiology.[26] Research carried out in pharmaceutical firms was considered to be largely of a practical or applied nature, and not contributing to the development of the fundamental science. Abel once explained to a colleague why he himself would not consider working on any problem suggested by a pharmaceutical firm:

Usually, problems of this nature could be worked out very well in the laboratories of the firms since they almost always concern questions of what I might call applied pharmacology. A pharmacologist of any training or ability should have so many problems of his own awaiting solution that he should not spend his time on matters of little theoretical importance for his science.[27]

Struggling to establish their discipline as an independent, basic science, the practitioners of pharmacology were especially anxious to avoid any taint of commercialism. Abel was so fastidious on this point that when he was elected as the Society's first president in 1908, he resigned from a special commission investigating the safety of saltpeter as a food additive. Although the commission was organized through the University of Illinois, it was funded in part by the American Packers Association. As the first president of an organization that banned industry pharmacologists from membership, Abel was concerned that his connection with the commission might be misunderstood, especially when he learned that rumors were circulating that he was "in the employ of the meat firms."[28]

In less than a decade, however, Abel began to soften his views on the question of industry pharmacologists. In early 1916, he wrote to a colleague in London that at the recent meeting (December, 1915) of ASPET in Boston he had sounded out some of the older members, such as Samuel Meltzer and Torald Sollmann, about the question of admitting pharmacologists in drug firms, such as Elijah Houghton, to membership in ASPET. He noted, however, that his colleagues were opposed to this step, believing that the time was not ripe for such an action. There was a feeling, he added, that "the drug house will not play 'fair' and will 'do us' at every opportunity."[29]

The issue was soon raised again, however, this time by Arthur Loevenhart of the University of Wisconsin. In 1918, Loevenhart discussed the question with Abel and, after receiving his support, submitted the following year an amendment to delete the membership restriction from the constitution. The amendment was originally scheduled to be discussed at a special meeting of the Society in April, 1919, but the issue was considered important and contro-

Arthur S. Loevenhart of the University of Wisconsin, who led the initial campaign to eliminate the American Society for Pharmacology and Experimental Therapeutics' membership ban on industrial pharmacologists (courtesy of the National Library of Medicine).

versial enough that it was decided to hold off consideration of it until the Society's regular meeting in Cincinnati the following December. Because of an unusually low attendance at that latter meeting however, no vote was taken on the amendment and it was referred to a special committee for evaluation. When a vote was finally taken at the 1920 meeting, the proposed amendment was unanimously defeated.[30] Abel was not in Chicago for the Society's meeting that year, and Loevenhart missed the business meeting due to a misunderstanding, so neither had an opportunity to speak on behalf of or vote for the amendment. Loevenhart vowed, however, to take up the fight again at some future date. Abel apparently still had mixed feelings about the issue, and admitted to a colleague after the meeting that he was less inclined to favor the amendment than he had been two years earlier.[31]

For the next two decades the issue remained a controversial one, periodically resurfacing to plague the Society. During this period, the proponents of changing the rule against industrial pharmacologists were unable to obtain the necessary four-fifths vote at an annual meeting to change the constitution on this point. There was, however, a growing sentiment to eliminate the restriction, culminating in the successful vote of 1941.

There were probably two major factors that contributed to the movement in the 1920s and 1930s to eliminate the ban against industrial pharmacologists. The first of these factors was the increase in the amount and quality of research being carried out by American pharmaceutical companies in the period between the two world wars. More and more pharmaceutical companies began to establish research facilities in the post World War I period, and some of the more prestigious companies began to become involved to some extent in basic research. As the image of research in the pharmaceutical industry improved, some of the stigma of being an industrial pharmacologist disappeared. A number of respected scientists, such as K. K. Chen at Lilly and Hans Molitor at Merck, followed in the footsteps of the fictional Max Gottlieb and joined the staff of pharmaceutical companies in the 1920s and 1930s. As pharmacologists of the stature of Chen and Molitor were excluded from membership in the Society, the pressure to change the constitution increased.[32]

In arguing the case for such a change, Abel wrote to Reid Hunt in 1927 that the large drug firms had a better attitude toward research than they did thirty years earlier.[33] In a letter to Sollmann in the same year, he noted that an increasing number of good pharmacologists were either not finding or not interested in academic positions and were pursuing careers with the larger pharmaceutical companies. Noting that he had originally been opposed to admitting industrial pharmacologists when the Society was founded, Abel added: "But times have changed and I wonder if we should not change with them."[34]

A second factor to be considered is the increasing involvement of academic pharmacologists with the drug industry in this period as consultants or in collaborative research agreements.[35] For example,

Loevenhart and later his successor at Wisconsin, Arthur Tatum, became involved in collaborative research on organic arsenical drugs with Parke, Davis and Company beginning in the 1920s.[36] In the early 1930s, University of Pennsylvania pharmacologist Alfred Newton Richards became a consultant to Merck on a regular basis and assisted them in developing an in-house program of pharmacological research.[37]

These consulting or collaborative arrangements were approached cautiously at first. Several colleagues, for example, wrote to Abel for counsel before undertaking such projects, seeking his opinion about the propriety of accepting payment from a pharmaceutical firm for performing some professional service.[38] Such arrangements became increasingly common and acceptable after World War I, and no doubt influenced the views of at least some pharmacologists about their industrial colleagues.

Even the traditional opposition on the part of many physicians and biomedical scientists to patenting medical discoveries began to erode in this period. By the mid-1930s at least a dozen universities were administering patents on medical discoveries by their faculty, further blurring the line between science and commerce.[39]

Those who supported changing the ASPET constitution to admit pharmacologists working for pharmaceutical firms argued that it was unnecessary to have a specific prohibition against these individuals. The Society's constitution and by-laws, it was claimed, provided adequate safeguards against the admission of unqualified members. Those who failed to meet the standards of the Society would be rejected, and any member who acted unethically or unprofessionally in some manner could be expelled under another provision of the constitution. Each applicant for membership should be judged individually on his or her merits, they argued, regardless of place of employment.[40]

Loevenhart complained that some, like Sollmann, criticized the low standards of pharmacological work in industry, but stood in the way of a major reform that might help to elevate these standards. Admitting industrial pharmacologists into ASPET would improve the chances of pharmaceutical firms to hire first-rate scientists, and company pharmacologists would benefit from their interaction with their academic colleagues within ASPET.[41]

Opponents of the change, however, were not satisfied with these arguments and continued to express concern that industrial pharmacologists might in time come to dominate the society and bend it to the needs of industry.[42] Robert Hatcher emphasized that the ideals of even the best scientists would gradually be broken down "by constant association with those who are in business with its insistent demand for financial success."[43] Some members tried to work out a compromise, whereby industry pharmacologists would be admitted as a new class of "associate members," but without the privilege of voting. But even this step went too far for some hard core opponents of any change, and some of those who favored eliminating the membership restriction were concerned that this procedure would still mark their industrial colleagues as second class citizens. The compromise effort never succeeded, and the issue remained unresolved.[44]

Some pharmacologists accepted the restriction on membership gracefully. For example, when K. K. Chen joined the staff of Eli Lilly and Company in 1929, he submitted his resignation to ASPET, expressing "a desire to comply with the ethics of the Society and leave it in good standing."[45]

Others employed by industrial firms were understandably disturbed by the restriction on membership. When pharmacologist David Macht, then at The Johns Hopkins University, contemplated accepting an offer of a research position from the Baltimore drug firm of Hynson, Westcott and Dunning in 1926, he wrote to Simon Flexner of the Rockefeller Institute to seek his advice. Macht wondered whether accepting such a position would ruin his scientific reputation and make it impossible for him to get back into academia.[46] Flexner replied, probably too optimistically:

Nowadays in this country it does not injure a man's reputation to go into a pharmaceutical firm of good standing. Men like Clowes with the Lillys, Anderson with Squibbs, and others, are in the scientific societies and are respected.[47]

These men were indeed often members of scientific societies, but were not, of course, admitted to ASPET. Macht did decide to accept the job offer, but soon he began to write to Flexner complaining about "the terrible and unjust discriminations made by other scientists more particularly medical men and pharmacologists against anyone connected with a commercial concern."[48] He was especially angered by what he called the "preposterous provision" in the constitution of the pharmacological society which excluded those employed in drug firms from membership.[49] British pharmacologist Henry Dale, who had himself worked for a pharmaceutical firm early in his career, would have sympathized with Macht on this point, for in 1933 he wrote to an American colleague that he regarded the attitude of ASPET towards industrial pharmacologists as "a piece of silly hypocrisy and pedantic snobbery."[50]

Although the rule remained in the constitution throughout the 1930s, one point at least was clarified during this decade. The question arose as to whether the phrase "in the permanent employ of a drug firm" included a paid consultation arrangement with a pharmaceutical company on a long-term basis. Pharmacologists had been consulting with drug firms before the 1930s, but the number of such arrangements increased, and some of these involved extensive consultation over a long period of time. The matter seems to have come to a head when A. N. Richards wrote to the Council of

ASPET on April 4, 1935, explaining that he had been acting as a paid consultant for Merck for three years, and that he felt it was his duty to bring this arrangement to the Council's attention because of the rule denying membership to those in the "permanent employ" of drug firms.[51]

The Council considered Richards' letter at its 1935 meeting, and agreed that the rule against industrial pharmacologists needed to be clarified with respect to consulting arrangements. A special committee was therefore established to study the problem, and in the meantime Richards was told that the Council did not feel that the arrangement he had with Merck violated the constitution.[52] It was recognized that by this time quite a few members were consulting with pharmaceutical firms.[53]

The committee, chaired by William deB. MacNider of the University of North Carolina, and including Abel as one of its members, recommended clarifying the two clauses in the constitution barring those "in the permanent employ of a drug firm" by adding the phrase "other than in the capacity of a consultant." Consulting arrangements would thus be explicitly excluded from the rule. They also proposed changing the term "drug firm" to "any organization concerned with the manufacture or sale of medicinal products." A majority of the members present at the 1936 annual meeting of ASPET (27 of 44) favored the amendment, but it did not receive the four-fifths majority needed for it to pass.[54] The same amendment was introduced again at the 1937 meeting, and this time it passed, although some members expressed concern about the advisability of passing an amendment "legalizing" consultation.[55] Meanwhile, there was no change in the status of pharmacologists whose sole or primary employer was a pharmaceutical company.

With the establishment of the Squibb Institute for Medical Research in 1938, its newly-appointed chief pharmacologist, Harry Van Dyke, tried a different approach to retaining his membership in the Society. Van Dyke pointed out that the Squibb Institute had been established for basic research, that it had its own board of scientific directors, and that it was relatively independent of the Squibb Company. He argued that he was therefore not really in the employ of a drug firm.[56] But the Society's Council refused to accept this argument. One officer commented:

Suppose Van Dyke would come out with a paper condemning, in no uncertain terms, one of E. R. Squibb and Sons' preparations. Van Dyke would lose his job. In other words, this means that Van Dyke is dependent upon E. R. Squibb and Sons for his livelihood.[57]

In any case, the Council felt that Van Dyke should not be treated differently from Chen, Molitor, and other industrial pharmacologists.[58]

The pressure to alter the constitution continued, however. In November of 1940, 24 distinguished members of the Society submitted another amendment to eliminate the ban on membership for industrial pharmacologists. The list of names included several who had been long-time opponents to amending the constitution for this purpose, such as Torald Sollmann and C. W. Edmunds.[59] It is not clear why these staunch foes of the amendment decided to change their position at this particular time, but certainly their switch played a key role in the eventual victory of the pro-amendment movement. On April 17, 1941, the 72 members present at the annual business meeting of ASPET unanimously approved amending the constitution to delete the restriction against industrial scientists, thus ending 33 years of a policy of discrimination against pharmacologists working for pharmaceutical firms.[60]

The improved image of industry science as pharmaceutical companies became more seriously involved in fundamental research, the entry of distinguished pharmacologists into the employ of industry, and the increasing involvement of academic scientists with industry as consultants all contributed to the eventual change in policy on the part of ASPET towards membership for industrial pharmacologists. The efforts of reputable drug firms to distance themselves from the manufacturers of quack patent medicines and increasing government regulation of the drug market may have also been factors in making the climate more favorable for the acceptance of industry pharmacologists by ASPET.

Over the past 40 years, the relationship between the Society and the pharmaceutical industry has become ever friendlier. In 1958, the Society established the membership category of corporate associates in an effort to secure financial support from industry.[61] There are currently some 40 to 50 corporate associates. It is not uncommon for an industrial scientist to be elected an officer, even President, of ASPET.[62] The situation is not significantly different from that of other scientific societies with significant industrial ties. The image of the pharmaceutical industry in the scientific community and the self-image of the pharmacology profession have improved to the point where a pharmacologist may accept a position in a pharmaceutical company without necessarily receiving the condemnation of his or her colleagues that the fictional Max Gottlieb did.

The concerns that motivated the founders of the American Society for Pharmacology and Experimental Therapeutics to institute their membership ban on industrial pharmacologists, however, have by no means disappeared. The increasing ties between industry and academia in recent times have caused renewed worries that the former may come to dominate the latter, and that science may become commercialized in the process. Some eighty years after the founding of ASPET, we are still searching for the appropriate balance of interaction between industrial and academic science. As John Swann noted in his recent book on the history of this interaction with respect to the pharmaceutical industry in the United States:

Universities, industry, and the public now have to decide how much collaboration is desirable for their needs; how much profit and impartiality they are willing to sacrifice; and which is the best possible course to satisfy the public good.[63]

Notes and References

The research for this paper was supported in part by NIH grant LM03300 from the National Library of Medicine.

1. Sinclair Lewis, *Arrowsmith* (New York: Harcourt Brace, 1925), p. 137.
2. See John Parascandola, "John J. Abel and the Early Development of Pharmacology at the Johns Hopkins University," *Bulletin of the History of Medicine* 56 (1982): 512–527.
3. K. K. Chen, "Meetings," in K. K. Chen, ed., *The American Society for Pharmacology and Experimental Therapeutics, Incorporated: The First Sixty Years, 1908–1969* (Bethesda, MD: American Society for Pharmacology and Experimental Therapeutics, 1969), pp. 5–11.
4. Ellsworth Cook, "Revisions of the Constitution and Bylaws," in Chen, *American Society* (n. 3), pp. 175–177, 184.
5. Undated draft of a letter from Reid Hunt to a committee of the council of the American Society for Pharmacology and Experimental Therapeutics appointed to draw up a constitution and bylaws, copy attached to a letter from Hunt to John Abel, January 2, 1909, John J. Abel Papers, Alan Mason Chesney Medical Archives, Johns Hopkins University, Baltimore, MD. The Abel Papers also contain a revised draft of this committee letter (also undated), and it includes the same statement.
6. Ibid. The initial draft named only Hunt, Crawford and Abel, but the revised draft added Loevenhart.
7. Typescript draft of constitution of the American Society for Pharmacology and Experimental Therapeutics, undated, in notebook on "Correspondence, ASPET Origins, C. W. Edmunds Files," American Society for Pharmacology and Experimental Therapeutics Archives, Bethesda, MD.
8. Incomplete typescript draft of ASPET constitution, undated, ibid.; Cook, "Revisions" (n. 4), p. 175.
9. See, for example, the correspondence in the Edmunds Files, ASPET Archives (n. 7); minutes of the organizational (1908) and first annual (1909) meeting of ASPET, Minutes and Records, volume 1 (1908–1916), ASPET Archives (n. 7); and the extensive correspondence in the founding of the Society in the Abel Papers (n. 5).
10. The Association of Official Agricultural Chemists did not admit industrial chemists, but there was no explicit ban in their constitution against such individuals. The Association accepted as active members only chemists associated with one of three types of institutions: the United States Department of Agriculture; any national, state or provincial experiment station or college engaged in agricultural chemistry research; and any national, state or provincial body charged with the official control of fertilizers, feeds and other agricultural products. In-

dustrial chemists were not singled out for exclusion. Chemists who worked for municipal laboratories or private research foundations, for example, were also ineligible to become active members. See Association of Official Agricultural Chemists, *Golden Anniversary of the Association of Official Agricultural Chemists, 1884–1934* (Washington, D.C.: 1934?), p. 19.

11. Charles Browne and Mary Weeks, *A History of the American Chemical Society: Seventy-five Eventful Years* (Washington, D.C.: American Chemical Society, 1952); Herman Skolnick and Kenneth Reese, eds., *A Century of Chemistry: The Role of Chemists and the American Chemical Society* (Washington, D.C.: American Chemical Society, 1976).

12. American Physiological Society, *History of the American Physiological Society, Semicentennial, 1887–1937* (Baltimore: 1938), John Brobeck, Orr Reynolds and Toby Appel, *History of the American Physiological Society: The First Century, 1887–1937* (Bethesda, MD: American Physiological Society, 1987); Russell H. Chittenden, *The First Twenty-five Years of the American Society for Biological Chemists* (New Haven, CT: American Society of Biological Chemists, 1945).

13. Letter from Richards to Abel, April 1, 1933, Abel Papers (n. 5).

14. Minutes of the Council, 1939, American Physiological Society Archives, Bethesda, MD. I am indebted to Toby Appel for calling my attention to these minutes and providing me with a copy.

15. On patent medicine quackery in this period, see James Harvey Young, *The Toadstool Millionaires: A Social History of Patent Medicines in America before Federal Regulation* (Princeton, NJ: Princeton University Press, 1961).

16. Abel to Robert Hatcher, January 31, 1910, Abel Papers (n. 5).

17. Abel to L. R. Hudson, December 7, 1915, Abel Papers (n. 5).

18. For a discussion of this point, see John Swann, *Academic Scientists and the Pharmaceutical Industry: Cooperative Research in Twentieth-Century America* (Baltimore: Johns Hopkins University Press, 1988), pp. 30–32.

19. For information on membership, see the society histories cited in notes 3, 11 and 12.

20. Hatcher to Arthur Loevenhart, December 26, 1919, Box 3, Arthur Loevenhart Papers, University of Wisconsin Archives, Madison, WI.

21. Sollman to Abel, February 9, 1927, Abel Papers (n. 5). Abel himself commented that ". . . for reasons evident to all medical men, it is the intention of the founders to impose unusual restrictions upon its members in respect to their connection with drug firms and other industrial concerns, a step that has my unqualified approval." Abel to Edmund James, January 5, 1909, Abel Papers (n. 5).

22. Meltzer to Abel, October 31, 1910, Abel Papers (n. 5).

23. Hunt to Abel, February 28, 1927, Abel Papers (n. 5).

24. Minutes of the fifth (1913) annual meeting of ASPET, Minutes and Records, volume 1 (1908–1916), ASPET Archives (n. 7).

25. Abel to Irvine Page, November 3, 1926, Abel Papers (n. 5).

26. John Abel, "The Methods of Pharmacology, with Experimental Illustration," *Pharmaceutical Era* 7 (1892): 105.

27. Abel to William De B. MacNider, April 5, 1935, Abel Papers (n. 5).

28. Abel to Edmund James, January 5, 1909 and Abel to A. P. Matthews, January 4, 1909, Abel Papers (n. 5).

29. Abel to Arthur Cushny, January 25, 1916, Abel Papers (n. 5).
30. Loevenhart to Abel, January 28, 1918, March 14, 1919, January 9, 1920, Abel Papers (n. 5); C. W. Edmunds to Abel, March 6, 1919, January 9, 1920, January 5, 1921, Abel Papers (n. 5); minutes of 11th (1919) and 12th (1920) annual meeting of ASPET, Minutes and Records, volume 2 (1917–1927), ASPET Archives (n. 7).
31. C. W. Edmunds to Abel, January 5, 1921, and Abel to Edmunds, January 10, 1921, Abel Papers (n. 5).
32. I have discussed the development of research in the American pharmaceutical industry during this period elsewhere. See John Parascandola, "Industrial Research Comes of Age: The American Pharmaceutical Industry, 1920–1940," *Pharmacy in History* 27 (1985): 12–21. See also Swann, *Scientists and the Pharmaceutical Industry* (n. 18), pp. 9–56, and Jonathan Liebenau, *Medical Science and Medical Industry: The Formation of the American Pharmaceutical Industry* (Baltimore: Johns Hopkins University Press, 1987).
33. Abel to Hunt, January 25, 1927, Abel Papers (n. 5).
34. Abel to Sollmann, February 2, 1927, Abel Papers (n. 5).
35. For a discussion of the growing interaction between academic scientists and the pharmaceutical industry in this period, see Swann, *Scientists and the Pharmaceutical Industry* (n. 18).
36. Ibid., pp. 93–117. See also John Swann, "Arthur Tatum, Parke-Davis, and the Discovery of Mapharsen as an Antisyphilitic Agent," *Journal of the History of Medicine and the Allied Sciences* 40 (1985): 167–187.
37. Swann, *Scientists and the Pharmaceutical Industry* (n. 18), pp. 65–86.
38. Robert Hatcher to Abel, January 28, 1910, A. N. Richards to Abel, August 30, 1930, William deB. MacNider to Abel, May 29, 1931, Abel Papers (n. 5).
39. Swann, *Scientists and the Pharmaceutical Industry* (n. 18), p. 75.
40. See, e.g., "Proposed Amendment to the Constitution of the American Society for Pharmacology and Experimental Therapeutics," undated printed document, minutes of 12th (1920) annual meeting of ASPET, Minutes and Records, volume 2 (1917–1927), ASPET Archives (n. 7). A copy of this proposed amendment from the 1920 meeting is also attached to a letter from Arthur Hirschfelder to Abel, January 20, 1927, Abel Papers (n. 5).
41. Loevenhart to Abel, March 14, 1919, Abel Papers (n. 5).
42. See, e.g., Robert Hatcher to Abel, February 4, 1927, Abel Papers (n. 5).
43. Ibid.
44. Sollmann to Abel, February 9, 1927, Abel to Arthur Loevenhart, February 16, 1927, Abel to David Macht, March 1, 1927, Macht to Abel, March 2, 1927, Abel to Chauncey Leake, March 22, 1932, Abel Papers (n. 5).
45. Minutes of the 20th (1929) annual meeting of ASPET, Minutes and Records, volume 3 (1928–1934), ASPET Archives (n. 7).
46. Macht to Flexner, April 5, 1926, Simon Flexner Papers, American Philosophical Society, Philadelphia, PA.
47. Flexner to Macht, April 5, 1926, Flexner Papers (n. 46). The name of Clowes is misspelled "Clawes" in the letter.
48. Macht to Flexner, October 25, 1928, Flexner Papers (n. 46).
49. Macht to Flexner, January 12, 1927, Flexner Papers (n. 46).
50. Dale to A. N. Richards, April 6, 1933, Box 32, A. N. Richards Papers, University of Pennsylvania Archives, Philadelphia, PA. I am grateful to John Swann for calling my attention to this letter.

51. Richards to ASPET Council, April 4, 1935, Richards Papers (n. 50).
52. E. M. K. Geiling to Richards, April 26, 1936, Box 10, Richards Papers (n. 50); minutes of the 26th (1935) annual meeting of the ASPET Council, Minutes and Records, volume 4 (1935–1937), ASPET Archives (n. 7).
53. E. M. K. Geiling to ASPET members, January 16, 1937, Minutes and Records, volume 4 (1935–1937), ASPET Archives (n. 7).
54. Minutes of the 27th (1936) annual meeting of ASPET, Minutes and Records, volume 4 (1935–1937), ASPET Archives (n. 7).
55. Minutes of the 28th (1937) annual meeting of ASPET, Minutes and Records, volume 4 (1935–1937), ASPET Archives (n. 7).
56. Van Dyke to Charles Gruber, July 14, 1938 and Van Dyke to G. Philip Grabfield, November 21, 1938, minutes of the 30th (1938) annual meeting of the ASPET Council, Minutes and Records, volume 5 (1938–1939), ASPET Archives (n. 7).
57. Arthur Tatum to G. Grabfield, July 22, 1938, Arthur Tatum Papers, Box 2, University of Wisconsin Archives, Madison, WI.
58. Minutes of the 30th (1939) annual meeting of the ASPET Council, Minutes and Records, volume 5 (1938–1939), ASPET Archives (n. 7).
59. Petition to G. Grabfield, November 6, 1940, Minutes and Records, volume 6 (1940–1941), ASPET Archives (n. 7).
60. Minutes of the 32nd (1941) annual meeting of the ASPET Council, Minutes and Records, volume 6 (1940–1941), ASPET Archives (n. 7).
61. K. K. Chen, "Membership," in Chen, *American Society* (n. 3), pp. 151–152. On the establishment of the corporate associates program, see also Otto Krayer to A. Weston, November 18, 1958, Box 13, Chauncey Leake Papers, National Library of Medicine, Bethesda, MD.
62. For information on the recent activities and policies of ASPET, see the periodical *The Pharmacologist*.
63. Swann, *Scientists and the Pharmaceutical Industry* (n. 18), pp. 170–181; the quotation is from p. 181.

A Brief History of the Pharmaceutical Industry in Basel

by Renate A. Riedl

SWITZERLAND today is the world's seventh largest producer of pharmaceuticals and, because of its small domestic market, has proportionally the highest export quota for pharmaceutical products: medicines worth 6.5 billion Swiss francs, or about 90% of total production were exported in 1988. Of the 1500 active substances introduced worldwide between 1960 and 1980, 7.3% originated from Switzerland. In a current list giving the country of origin of the 100 top-selling drugs in the world-market, Switzerland, with 12%, is in fourth place behind the USA (35%), Great Britain, and West Germany (14%).

These figures are a measure of past achievements in the research sphere. The intensive work going on in the research laboratories today is directed towards discovering the drugs of the future. Statistics from the end of 1985, which rank pharmaceutical companies according to the number of active substances undergoing research and development, show three Swiss companies among the leading fifteen worldwide: Ciba-Geigy Ltd., Sandoz Ltd., and F. Hoffmann-La Roche & Co. Ltd., all three having their headquarters in Basel.

The drugs of tomorrow must, of course, be financed today. The research activities of the Swiss pharmaceutical industry are financed exclusively from self-generated funds, i.e., 100% risk capital. In 1986, expenditure on research and development in the chemical-pharmaceutical industry was way ahead of that in other industries. Worldwide investments in research and development by Swiss industry totalled 7.9 billion Swiss francs. The portion invested by the chemical-pharmaceutical industry was 4.2 billion francs (54%), of which more than two-thirds was accounted for by the pharmaceutical sector. The three Basel companies mentioned above spend between 10 and 15% of their annual worldwide revenue from sales on

Head of Corporate Archives, Sandoz Ltd., 4002 Basel, Switzerland.

research and development. In 1988 their combined research and development expenditures for pharmaceuticals alone amounted to 2.2 billion Swiss francs or 17% of their combined pharmaceutical sales. In a broad analysis of the significance of the Swiss pharmaceutical industry in terms of the domestic economy, the fact should not be overlooked that it provides some 30,000 jobs, representing approximately half of the total workforce of the chemical industry.

The astonishing thing about these figures is that they pertain to a small country which, at first glance, appears to possess none of the assets necessary to produce successful export industries: It has virtually no natural resources; labor costs in Switzerland are among the highest in the world; moreover, the Swiss franc has for years been appreciating against almost all currencies, of primary importance being its upward revaluation against the currencies of major competitors such as the United States, West Germany, Japan, France, Great Britain, and Italy.

Handicapped by these adverse factors—reliance on exports, high labor costs, and the strong external value of the Swiss franc—the Swiss pharmaceutical industry can only maintain and sharpen its competitive edge in international markets if it is capable—as in the past—of developing and selling innovative, high value added products. The Swiss pharmaceutical industry—and here we refer primarily to the three "majors" of the Basel chemical industry which will be the subject of this essay—has, in the past, repeatedly demonstrated its ability to adapt to the changing conditions of the market and the business environment. In spite of the above-mentioned disadvantages of Switzerland as an exporting base, it was able to consolidate and improve its position in the world pharmaceuticals market.

A City and its Industry

Today, the pharmaceutical industry in Switzerland consists of about 400 firms (companies with manufacturing facilities (85), as well as trading companies, distributors, and representatives), though only seven of these employ more than 500 people. Three of them figure among the world's leading companies in the chemical-pharmaceutical sector: Ciba-Geigy Ltd., Sandoz Ltd., and F. Hoffmann-La Roche & Co. Ltd. All three were founded in Basel where they still have their headquarters.

Basel, in the northwestern corner of Switzerland, with France and Germany as its immediate neighbors, is today one of the world's leading centers of pharmaceutical research. Nowhere in the world does one find so many researchers from this field concentrated in what is only a middle-sized city. The chemical-pharmaceutical industry is also one of the most important generators of prosperity in the region—as an economic analysis published in 1986 shows.

Around 50% of the basic creation of wealth in the area can be ascribed to this industry. Today, Basel and the chemical industry are notions that have become inseparable—so much so that it is easily forgotten that this "economic marriage" was first formed in the middle of the nineteenth century.

The modern city of Basel is one of the biggest and most important trading centers in Switzerland. But the origins of Basel as an economic and cultural center can be traced back as far as the Middle Ages. At that time, the city was an important focus of trade and commerce and a major crossroads on the north-south transalpine route, a position it owed largely to its Rhine bridge, which was the last crossing point until well down the lower reaches of the river at Cologne. With the foundation of its university in 1460 (the nucleus of which had existed—with interruptions—since its original establishment by the Ecumenical Council in 1444) a cultural and scientific dimension was added to the city's influence as a business center.

Besides the early pre-eminence of Basel as a center of commerce and communications and as a university city, another factor that contributed to the development of its manufacturing industries was the fact that, in the wake of the Thirty Years' War and the campaigns of Louis XIV, the merchants of the neutral Helvetic Confederation and the city of Basel were able successfully to challenge their French rivals' domination of the German market. The main architects of this trade boom were the refugees who had emigrated to the city during the upheavals of the Reformation and Counter-Reformation. The reformed city of Basel offered a safe haven and opportunities of advancement to numerous religious refugees who, for the most part, hailed from internationally renowned centers of high-quality textile manufacture: Upper Italy, France, and the Netherlands. They revolutionized the structure of the native textile industry, albeit for a long time in conflict with the restrictive practices of the local guilds. The first wave of immigrants, who were largely responsible for creating the industries that blossomed in the city during the eighteenth and nineteenth centuries, arrived between 1565 and 1601. The second period of immigration was at the time of the Thirty Years' War. In contrast to the refugees of the sixteenth century, who were mostly skilled artisans, this second wave consisted largely of merchants. They cultivated their valuable network of commercial contacts to the benefit of Basel's trade position. The last great influx of immigrants followed the revocation of the Edict of Nantes in 1685.

For two hundred years, the textile—or more precisely the silk-ribbon—industry founded by these refugees dominated the city's economy, reaching its zenith in the mid-nineteenth century. In 1856, an English chemist, William Henry Perkin (1838–1907), accidentally discovered that dyestuffs can be made from coal tar, a byproduct of lighting gas production. His discovery marked the be-

ginning of the synthetic dyestuffs industry. This "waste" product
suddenly became a much sought after raw material. Thanks to the
textile industry, the nascent coal-tar dye industry in Basel found a
well developed infrastructure already at hand, allowing it to establish
a leading position in the rapidly expanding world market. Like the
machine-building industry, which evolved from being a mere aux-
iliary trade servicing the textile factories to become the most important sector of the Swiss economy, the chemical industry in Basel
is, in a sense, the progeny of silk-ribbon and textile manufacture.

Was Basel in the mid-nineteenth century an ideal site for the
chemical industry? The city appears predestined for its role by a
number of propitious circumstances. As we have already said, Basel
was the center of a prosperous silk-ribbon industry; but neighboring
Alsace and South Baden, with their thriving textile factories and
cloth-printing firms, were also a natural market for dyestuffs and
textile auxiliaries. Moreover, Switzerland at that time had no restrictive patent legislation—quite unlike the situation that existed,
for example, in France. In order to produce dyestuffs without hindrance, using the new technology, a large number of French chemists

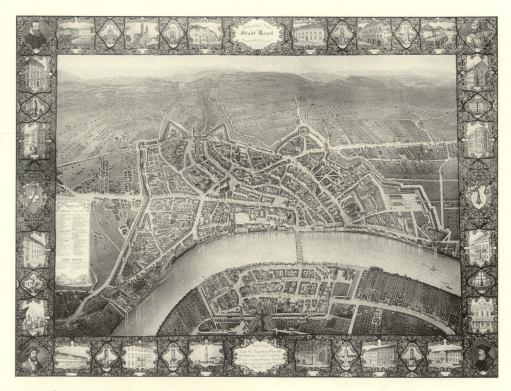

Map of Basel, 1847. Print by Friedrich Maehly.

and entrepreneurs emigrated to Switzerland, taking their capital and their know-how with them. Many of these "patent refugees" chose to set up their new enterprises in Basel, just across the frontier. Another factor that certainly influenced their choice of location was the presence of the Rhine, which provided the water for the dyestuffs manufacturing process and—in keeping with the notions prevailing at that time—an outfall for their waste water. Other factors undoubtedly contributed: for example, the plentiful supply of capital in a city with a rich trading and banking tradition, the cultural climate of the ancient university town, and not least, good communications. Taken singly, none of these factors was crucial; taken together, they were decisive.

From Dyes to Fine Chemicals and Pharmaceuticals

We have so far spoken more about dyestuffs than pharmaceuticals. With the possible exception of sulphuric acid manufacture, the beginnings of industrial chemistry were entirely congruent with the development of dyestuff chemistry. However, not long after Perkin's discovery, there was a general realization that coal tar was also suitable as a starting substance for certain basic pharmaceutical products. But only at a later stage, towards the end of the nineteenth century, did individual firms extend the scope of their activities beyond the dyestuffs and chemicals businesses. The First World War exposed the vulnerability of the Basel dyestuffs industry: dependence on imported raw materials, problems with distribution, with coordination of foreign affiliates and, after the war, a fierce competitive struggle with the German, French, British, and rising American dye industries. The dependence of dyestuffs manufacturers on the health of the textile industry created additional problems. Against this stark background, the opportunities offered by the development of pharmaceutical specialties began to beckon.

With the exception of a few firms that started life as pharmacies, most of the major companies operating in the Swiss pharmaceutical sector today evolved through diversification of the early dye works. This is true of Ciba, Geigy (now Ciba-Geigy), and Sandoz. Only Hoffmann-La Roche differs from the other Basel companies in that it concentrated, from its earliest beginnings in 1896, on the production of pharmaceutical specialties, at that time considered a high risk venture. At Ciba, pharmaceutical production began as early as 1889, developing slowly and prudently. Sandoz, though it started manufacturing nonpatented basic pharmaceutical substances in 1895, did not commit itself fully to this sector until 1917 when a separate pharmaceuticals department was established. In terms of scientific achievement, success came rapidly; the economic benefits took ten years to become apparent, but when eventually they did, the magnitude was quite unexpected. At Geigy, entry into the phar-

maceuticals business followed much later, despite the fact that the
company, with its expertise in the area of dyestuff extraction, was
well placed to start extracting other substances, such as alkaloids.
The first Geigy pharmaceuticals appeared in 1938.

This reluctance to move into the pharmaceuticals market, a step
that for some time aroused controversy in certain quarters, is more
understandable if one considers that the drug business was initially
a loss-maker. In the early years, pharmaceutical research had to be
financed out of revenue from the sale of dyes. Moreover, at that
time the dyes business had a much better image than pharmaceuticals. It had the character of a large-scale industry: dyestuffs and
chemicals were sold in huge tonnages to important firms. In the
pharmaceuticals business, by contrast, the big dye producers saw
themselves reduced, as it were, to the level of small traders, selling
goods on a piecemeal basis to pharmacists and physicians. Furthermore, extracts from natural sources—the origin of most early
pharmaceuticals—were considered inferior to synthetic chemicals.
Nor was the quality of the drugs produced in those days comparable
with that of present-day formulations. Indeed, none of the early
drugs would stand the least chance of obtaining official approval for
market release under modern conditions. The early patent remedies
were either of low potency or, if stronger, caused serious side effects.
Attention to purity was lax; it was only after instrumental analysis
reached a certain level of sophistication that modern standards could
be introduced. But many years were to pass before industrial drug
research attained a status equivalent to that enjoyed by university-
level research.

Today, the significance of the Basel chemical companies in the
scientific domain is as uncontested as their economic prowess. With
a combined turnover of more than 36 billion Swiss francs, the three
leading groups—transnational corporations operating in the same
business environment—have grown increasingly to resemble one another. A telling indication of the present situation is that, in Basel,
notwithstanding the natural and necessary rivalry of the three
groups, they are referred to as "Kollegialfirmen" (i.e., "colleague
companies"). In examining the "curricula vitae" of the original four
majors, today the "Big Three" of the Basel chemical industry, it is
our intention above all to point up the differences in their respective
histories. These are sometimes obscured by the collective term
"Basel chemical industry." To do justice to the title of this essay,
we will concentrate our attention on the development of the pharmaceuticals sector within the Basel companies.

F. Hoffmann-La Roche & Co. Ltd.

Unlike the other Basel firms, Ciba, Geigy (now Ciba-Geigy), and
Sandoz, which all began as textile dye manufacturers, Hoffmann-
La Roche was founded as a pharmaceutical company.

View of the northwestern corner of Basel with Sandoz Ltd. on the left bank of the Rhine and Ciba-Geigy Ltd. on the right.

Fritz Hoffmann-La Roche (1868–1920). Founder of F. Hoffmann-La Roche & Co., Ltd.

In 1894, Fritz Hoffmann-La Roche (1868–1920), along with Max Carl Traub, took over the drug-making operation of a pharmacist's shop and in the same year founded the limited partnership Hoffmann-Traub & Co., which, in 1896, after the withdrawal of one partner was transformed into F. Hoffmann-La Roche & Co.

The firm's foundation was the product of an entrepreneurial concept. Hoffmann was one of the first to recognize the nature of the pharmaceutical specialty. At a time when the vast majority of medicines were individually prescribed by doctors and then made up by hand in pharmacies, he foresaw the great revolution in industrially manufactured pharmaceutical specialties. He recognized that the future belonged to products which were of consistent composition, effect, and quality, ready for use at all times and labelled with a brand name. He also had definite ideas about the way in which these products should be sold: medicines also need promoting if they are to sell. At that time, advertisements for drugs were a novelty; it was advertising that made the success of products such as "Sirolin," a cough syrup, one of the earliest Roche products, upon whose sales the growth of the company in the early decades was founded. Besides the general public, Hoffmann's advertising was also designed as information for the medical profession. Hoffmann thought it important for his staff to get scientific articles published in medical journals. He published his own scientific organ, a venture then unique in Europe.

Until shortly before the turn of the century, the number of specialties manufactured by Roche was modest and so, too, was the turnover. All that changed abruptly in 1897 when a water-soluble form of guaiacol was successfully produced by means of a sulfonation process, a product that was sold under the brand name Thiocol. However, it was only to make a commercial impact as the basic ingredient of the cough syrup Sirolin, which sold in huge quantities and remained on the market until 1963. These two products were joined in 1904 by Digalen, an extract of the purple foxglove (*Digitalis purpurea*) used in the treatment of cardiovascular disorders. This latter drug launched Roche into the forefront of the pharmaceutical industry. Digalen remained a standard medication until the twenties when it was supplanted by the glycosides that resulted from the research of Professor Arthur Stoll (Sandoz). Five years later, Pantopon was developed, a preparation containing the potent alkaloids of opium in the form of hydrochloric salts, which opened up new possibilities for analgesic treatment.

The advent of these drugs ushered in a new era for the firm. Modern production facilities were built. The company's foreign operations in particular experienced a period of dramatic growth. From the very beginning, Fritz Hoffmann's vision had been to create a worldwide network of companies. But with the outbreak of the First World War, his enterprise was put to a severe test. The main manufacturing plant in German Grenzach, just across the border from Switzerland, was closed down by the German authorities. As a result, the company faced enormous difficulties, which the opening of a Swiss production plant could do little to assuage. However, the severest blow was the loss of the Russian market, which accounted for one fifth of prewar sales. The firm was saved from collapse by

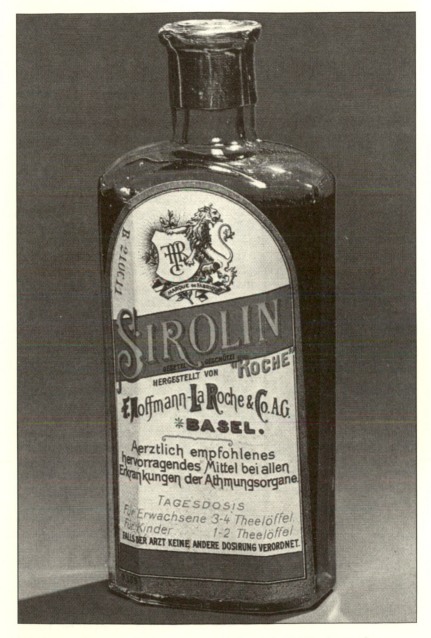

Sirolin cough-syrup, the first commercially successful Roche product.

transformation into a public limited (joint stock) company, established in 1919 with a capital stock of 4 million Swiss francs.

In the period between the wars, which saw the triumphant progress of pharmacotherapy, Roche research enjoyed a marked upturn in its fortunes. The head of research during that period, Dr. Markus Guggenheim (1885–1970), who had worked in the firm since 1910, was an important figure in the development of biochemistry. The range of his scientific achievement is enormous. As late as the nineteen sixties, drugs were being introduced whose structure he had analyzed before the First World War. In 1913, for instance, he had illuminated the structure of the amino acid L-dopa. In 1970, it was introduced as Larodopa, the first antiparkinsonian agent, soon to be followed by Madopar, a drug with even greater pharmacological efficacy.

Guggenheim's work also had some impact in the field of vitamins research. It helped prepare the ground for the total synthesis of ascorbic acid (vitamin C), accomplished by Professor Tadeus Reichstein in 1933. Roche developed commercial production techniques for vitamin C, on the strength of which it has since played a leading role in industrial-scale manufacture of vitamins. Another turning point in the history of the "vitamin epoch" was the synthesis of vitamin A by Dr. Otto Isler. Vitamin research, a dominant activity for decades, was, both scientifically and economically, of paramount significance for Roche. There was growing recognition of the importance of vitamins for disease prophylaxis and increasing physical performance. A series of major pharmaceutical specialties was developed in the light of these discoveries.

Between the wars, hypnotics and analgesics played an increasingly important role among the Roche specialties. One of the few "classic" drugs to survive from that period is Prostigmin (neostigmine), introduced in 1931, which is used to reverse flaccid paralysis caused by anaesthetic muscle relaxants in surgery. It is also indicated for reduction of intraocular pressure as well as for lowering heart rate in tachycardia.

In 1952, exactly seventy years after the discovery of the tubercle bacillus by Robert Koch, the introduction of Rimifon marked a turning point in the fight against tuberculosis. The active substance had been synthesized as early as 1912, but it was not until 1950 that its efficacy was recognized in the Roche laboratories. The discovery of the antitubercular activity of isonicotinic acid hydrazide caused something of a sensation in the world of medicine and is a milestone in the struggle against what is, medically and socially, one of the most pernicious human diseases.

The incidental mood-elevating effect of Rimifon that was observed in tuberculosis patients aroused interest in psychotropic substances and led to the development of a new group of drugs, the monoamine oxidase inhibitors. Another class of antidepressants emerged from imipramine, a drug that was initially developed for use against allergies and Parkinson's disease. The third group of psychotropics—and for Roche the most important—was the minor tranquilizers, which have been used especially in outpatient treatment. Librium and Valium, which belong to the benzodiazepine group of substances, were introduced in 1961 and 1963 respectively. They represent a key chapter in the history of Hoffmann-La Roche. Their impact on the company has been enormous and the consequences have been manifold. For many years, they were the most widely sold drugs in the world, a success that no one, not even at Roche, could have anticipated, but which also brought unexpected problems. The reproach that Roche, with its price policy, had abused the dominant market position it held was finally laid to rest after many years of legal wrangling.

The field of endogenous, physiological substances that Roche has been continuously investigating since Guggenheim's day, is one of great potential. Strong public interest has been aroused by the enormous medical potential of immunological modulators, such as the interferons, whose characterization and production were made possible by important advances in biotechnology. A major contribution to this development was made by the two basic research institutes established by Roche in the late sixties, and still funded by the company. At the Roche Institute of Molecular Biology in Nutley, N.J., essential preliminary work was carried out on the genetically engineered recombination method for biotechnological production of the first interferon. The discovery of monoclonal antibodies, a development which is increasingly being recognized as one of the major biological and medical breakthroughs, was made at the Basel Institute for Immunology. The basic research conducted at the Basel institute which elucidated the structure and regulatory mechanisms of the body's defense system has achieved worldwide recognition. For this work, Niels K. Jerne and Georges Köhler—along with Cesar Milstein in London—received in 1984 the Nobel Prize for Physiology and Medicine. Nineteen eighty-six was another memorable year for genetic engineering research at Roche: Roferon-A, an alpha interferon produced by genetic engineering techniques, was approved for use in the therapy of hair-cell leukemia. Interferon has meanwhile gained the status of a prototype, providing a model for the conduct of medical research into new immunobiological substances and their therapeutic use.

Today, the Roche Group is active in the areas of pharmaceuticals, vitamins, and fine chemicals, diagnostics, perfumes and flavorings, crop protection agents, as well as instruments and liquid crystals. In 1988 the company had a total workforce of 49,671, of whom 10,645 are employed in Switzerland. For the last fiscal year it recorded total sales of 8,694 million Swiss francs.

Sandoz Ltd.

In 1885, the businessman Edouard Sandoz (1853–1928) and the chemist Alfred Kern (1850–1893) decided to establish a factory in Basel for the manufacture of synthetic dyestuffs. One year later, on 1 July 1886, "Chemische Fabrik Kern & Sandoz" started production at the site now occupied by the group's headquarters. Thanks to the new dyestuffs developed by Alfred Kern, the small company enjoyed rapid growth. Following the sudden death of Alfred Kern in 1893, Edouard Sandoz ran the company alone until its transformation, in 1895, into a public limited company; this bore the name "Chemische Fabrik vormals Sandoz" until 1939 when it was changed to Sandoz Ltd. Today, the Sandoz Group is a multinational corporation with over 170 subsidiaries in 55 countries. Sales in 1989 totalled 12,497 million Swiss francs of which 5,667 million francs (45%) were generated by the Pharmaceuticals Division. More than 50,000 employees, of whom about 7,400 work in Switzerland, work in the divisions which cover pharmaceuticals, chemicals, agrochemicals, seeds, nutrition, and construction chemicals.

For thirty years, the company concentrated mainly on the manufacture of dyestuffs and textile chemicals. But even before the turn of the century, dyestuffs production was complemented by a modest range of basic pharmaceuticals and saccharine. In 1895, Sandoz joined the antipyrine convention and immediately took up the manufacture of this highly effective fever-reducing agent. It had been launched by Hoechst in 1884 and was the synthetic pharmaceutical success story of the last century; moreover, it was under patent protection in only a few countries. However, market conditions were extremely volatile and the antipyrine convention collapsed as early as 1898. After a lapse of ten years, it enjoyed a revival, but only temporarily.

During those years, Sandoz tried to complement its antipyrine business by repeating the same pattern with other successful drugs. One result of this was the codeine convention which was signed in 1902. Later, the company experimented with chocolate cough sweets containing guaiacol, and a laxative in biscuit form. However, these products do not seem to have met with much success. It appears that the dye manufacturers lacked the experience or the interest necessary to launch pharmaceutical products.

During the First World War, the general shortage of drugs compelled Sandoz to concentrate its efforts on the manufacture of aminopyrine, phenolphthalein, antipyrine, and barbital, all nonpatented active substances which could be produced and distributed on a commercial scale. The run on prices for basic pharmaceuticals, which began before the end of the war, confirmed the management of Sandoz in their decision to develop their own patent-protected drugs, with the promise of more favorable market conditions. In

1917, the Board of Directors made a decision that proved crucial for the future of the concern. In order to broaden the company's base, the better to meet increasing pressure from competition within the dyes sector that was expected after the end of the war, the board decided to create a new department for pharmaceutical specialties. This was the most momentous event in the 104-year history of Sandoz.

The young man entrusted with the job of building up the new department was Professor Arthur Stoll (1887–1971), a biochemist. As assistant to the Nobel prizewinner Richard Willstätter, he had already made a name for himself with his work on chlorophylls and enzymes. His main contribution to the development of the pharmaceutical industry in Basel consists in the important role he played in helping to raise the nascent industrial drug research departments to the high level of university research. He also devised a method for isolating active substances in pure form from traditional medicinal plants, thus making it possible to produce drugs that could be accurately dosed.

Stoll's first project was with ergot, a fungal growth which affects various cereals and wild grasses. It had already been used for centuries as a herbal medicine to promote uterine contractions during labor. In 1918 Stoll succeeded for the first time in producing a pure, crystalline, homogeneous alkaloid, to which he gave the name ergotamine. In 1921 this substance came onto the market as Gynergen, at that time the most effective means of controlling postpartum hemorrhage. But pharmaceutical researchers at Sandoz in the twenties and thirties did not confine themselves to the study of ergot. Their investigations of squill (Scilla maritima) and white foxglove (Digitalis lanata) resulted in the development of a series of cardioactive glycosides. Another product developed during this pioneering age of the pharmaceutical industry was a well tolerated, injectable calcium formulation for the treatment of calcium deficiency and the disorders that result from it. Calcium-Sandoz, a novel calcium compound that came onto the market in 1929, became the foundation for modern calcium therapy.

In the 1940s, ergot research enjoyed a revival: intensive research led to the extraction of new pharmaceutical substances with different modes of action. One discovery made at that time was the inhibitory effect of ergotamine on the autonomous nervous system and its therapeutic benefits for migraine sufferers. This resulted, in 1949, in the introduction of Hydergine, a combination of three derivatives of the ergotoxine alkaloids, initially used to treat blood pressure disorders, and later mainly administered in the therapy of age-related cerebral insufficiency. Today, it is still one of the biggest selling Sandoz products. Parlodel is another product of ergot research, originally used in the treatment of hormonal disorders. In recent years, it has also been used in Parkinson's disease.

Dr. Albert Hofmann (b. 1906), the Sandoz chemist, who discovered the effects of LSD in the course of his ergot research.

It was not until the fifties that the search for potentially interesting active substances was extended to purely synthetic compounds. An early discovery, still used successfully today, was the neuroleptic Mellaril, a derivative of chlorpromazine, introduced in 1960 for the treatment of mental and emotional disorders. The treatment of allergic disorders was another area that benefited from this research. Visken, a drug from the family of beta-blockers, which are used in the treatment and prophylaxis of hypertensive and coronary illnesses, similarly enhanced the growing reputation of Sandoz research. The nineteen fifties also saw the beginning of research into the hormones of the diencephalon (particularly of the hypothalamus) and the pituitary gland (hypophysis). Efforts to map the complex molecular structure of these substances and reproduce them by synthetic means led to the development of a pure form of oxytocin, the natural hormone that stimulates uterine contraction during labor. The structure of the hormone calcitonin, which plays a key role in calcium metabolism, was also decoded. Not long afterwards, it was discovered that calcitonin from salmon is a much more potent substance and in 1974 it was launched commercially as Calcitonin Sandoz for the treatment of bone decalcification. Sandoz also made a valuable contribution to the fight against infectious diseases. The Austrian firm Biochemie, a Sandoz subsidiary, developed the first orally effective penicillin.

With the discovery and development of cyclosporin A, a metabolite isolated from a fungus, Sandoz research earned worldwide recognition in the field of immunology. It was soon discovered that the substance had a powerful and hitherto unknown effect on the immune system. The active substance specifically inhibits immunological rejection of transplanted organs. Under the brand name Sandimmun, this drug has brought a new surge of activity in the field of organ and bone-marrow transplantation and ushered in a new generation of immunosuppressives.

During the past seven decades—pioneering years, years of consolidation and momentous discoveries—Sandoz research has not only produced numerous valuable and essential drugs, but also built up a huge store of knowledge and experience in areas where the company is an acknowledged world leader. A brief survey of these achievements takes in the chemistry of natural substances, particularly of ergot alkaloids, peptides, and certain aspects of microbiology; in respect to the biological aspects of therapy mention must be made of cardio- and cerebrovascular disorders, psychiatry and neurology, geriatric medicine, endocrinology and immunology; great efforts have been made in the increasingly important area of biotechnology. The company has also initiated new forms of cooperation between academic and industrial research with the opening of a clinical-pharmacological ward in the university hospital in Vienna and the Sandoz Institute for Medical Research at University College London.

J.R. Geigy Ltd.

Johann Rudolf Geigy-Gemuseus (1733–1793), who established himself in 1758 as a crude-drug merchant, can be regarded as a forerunner of the modern chemical industry in Basel. He imported mainly medicinal substances and natural dyestuffs, but also spices and colonial goods, which he supplied to dyers, apothecaries, and grocer's shops. A list of goods includes coffee, tea, cocoa, various spices and diverse types of rubber, pigments such as indigo and exotic dyewoods. He also dealt in popular remedies of the time such as cinchona bark, opium, ipecacuanha, and rhubarb. In view of the general upswing in the textile industry, the following generations of the Geigy family concentrated more and more on the dye trade, dealing mainly in indigo and madder. Then, in 1833, the family installed its own dyewood press to process the exotic logwoods, yellowwoods, and redwoods. The final step from trading company to industrial firm followed in 1858 with the construction of their own dyeworks, which included actual extraction of pigments by boiling dyewoods in water.

In 1859, three years after Perkin's sensational discovery of synthetic dyestuffs, Geigy began to experiment with the manufacture of fuchsin, then the most prized of all dyes, and a range of other coal tar dyestuffs followed. Trading activities were increasingly pushed into the background in favor of industrial manufacture. In keeping with tradition, export soon occupied a key position and a network of sales agents and representatives soon extended throughout Europe, America, and parts of Asia. In 1901, the firm was transformed into a limited company. It was about this time that the first proposal to take up the production of pharmaceuticals was made. However, despite the fact that certain farsighted personalities were convinced of the necessity of extending the scope of the firm's activities beyond the traditional dyestuffs sector, they were unable to win over the majority of the board of directors.

In the aftermath of the First World War, the competitive situation in the dyes sector was radically transformed: the German dyestuffs manufacturers merged to form the powerful IG Farben combine, and national chemical industries grew up in the USA, Great Britain, France, Italy, and Japan. In 1918, the Basel firms, Ciba, Sandoz and Geigy, responded by forming the "Basler Interessengemeinschaft," an interest group which was to continue in existence until 1950. Under the terms of this agreement, the three partners were to pool their gross profits and divide them up in accordance with fixed quotas. Each company was assigned particular fields of activity, a restriction which for Geigy proved both a hindrance—since the opportunities for diversification were difficult to size up—and a boon, because it obliged the company to shed something of its conservativeness and expand, at least within the limits of its traditional activities. To begin with, Geigy expanded in the direction of textile chemicals and synthetic tanning agents. Soon, other opportunities presented themselves: inherent in textile finishing was the problem of fabric protection. What good were the finest dyes if the wool fibers were threatened by insect damage?

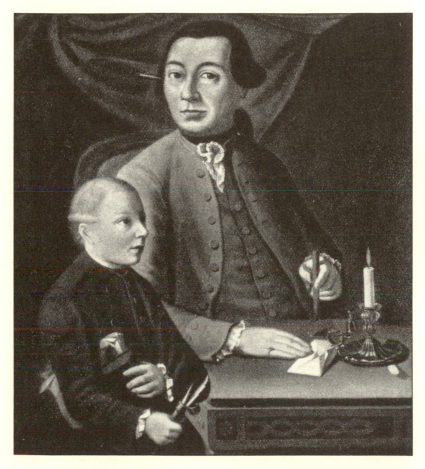

Johann Rudolf Geigy (1733–1793) and his son Hieronymus.

The techniques used in developing the first washable mothproofing treatment opened the door to a whole new field of activity. On the one hand, it was a bridge to the manufacture of pesticides generally, but also to the new opportunities offered by pharmaceutical specialties. Shortly after the outbreak of the Second World War, Geigy achieved a worldwide breakthrough with the discovery of the insecticide properties of dichlorodiphenyltrichloroethane—DDT for short—for which Dr. Paul Müller received the 1948 Nobel Prize for Physiology and Medicine. In the meantime, this pioneer product, whose value was undisputed at the time of its discovery and subsequent widespread usage, has been superceded by a new generation of insecticides that combine greater efficacy with more rapid biodegradability.

Geigy did not establish its pharmaceuticals department until 1938, some fifty years after CIBA. Initially, pharmaceutical research at Geigy was carried out mainly by chemists who had gained their experience synthesizing dyestuffs and textile auxiliaries. From 1941 onwards, it was carried out on a broader basis, involving scientists whose background was in pharmacology and medicine. In that same year, continuing earlier research in the bacteriological field, Geigy launched their first product onto the market, a surface disinfectant which, among other applications, was suitable as a replacement for iodine tincture. This early phase of pharmaceutical activity also saw the development of sulfonamide formulations.

However, the real breakthrough for Geigy in the pharmacological-medical field came with the discovery of the antirheumatic properties of Butazolidin. With Tanderil, which is used as an analgesic with antiinflammatory activity, and above all Voltaren, it is one of the most effective anti-inflammatory drugs available today. In view of the many unsolved problems presented by the treatment of rheumatic illness it is still an area of intensive research at Ciba-Geigy. A second priority area was that of psychotropic drugs, especially the antidepressants. In 1958, Geigy introduced Tofranil (imipramine hydrochloride), the first drug with mood-elevating properties to be used in psychopharmacological therapy. In 1969, the company broached the field of tropical medicine with a sulfonamide that proved particularly effective against the pathogen responsible for leprosy. Finally, with a beta-blocker introduced in 1970, Geigy made its own contribution to modern cardiovascular therapy. At the time of its merger with the CIBA group in 1970, the range of Geigy activities covered the dyestuffs, pigments, chemicals and plastics additives, pharmaceuticals, and agrochemicals sectors.

CIBA Ltd.

The foundation of CIBA was a direct consequence of the discovery of aniline dyestuffs. The discovery was made—as we have already mentioned—in 1856 by the young William Henry Perkin, assistant to the famous chemist August W. Hofmann at the Royal College of Chemistry in London, while attempting to synthesize quinine from aniline. After oxidizing crude aniline with bichromate he found, instead of the desired medicinal substance, a small quantity of a violet pigment, which he was able to extract from the oxidation product. The pigment proved capable of dyeing silk, without first treating it with a mordant, in sumptuous violet hues of unprecedented beauty. Perkin called his mauve-colored dyestuff Mauvein and was soon engaged in the commercial exploitation of his discovery, building the world's first aniline dye works at Greenford Green in London.

Not long afterwards, a textile chemist of Lyon, Emmanuel Verguin, discovered another way of synthesizing an aniline dye. Verguin oxidized crude aniline with stannic chloride, obtaining a brilliant bluish red, which he called Fuchsin, a dye that was subsequently to prove much more important than Perkin's Mauvein. Verguin sold his process in 1858 to the great Lyon silk dyeworks of Renard Frères et Franc. Fuchsin was a spectacular success; silk dyers vied eagerly for the new dye. Fantastic prices, up to 1500 Swiss francs (in the money of the time) per kilogram, were demanded—and paid.

It was from Lyon that Alexandre Clavel (1805–1873) had come to Basel in 1838 to take over the running of a silk dyeworks. Through his family connections to one of the proprietors of Renard Frères et Franc he was able, in 1859, to obtain a license for the fuchsin process, paying the sum of 100,000 francs. His fuchsin plant began production that same year. Until 1864, Clavel manufactured the dye at his works situated close to the center of the city. A growing chorus of protest from the population complaining of air, soil, and other forms of pollution eventually culminated in a ban on production by the local health authorities. The factory had to be moved to the outskirts of the town. He built his new factory on the Rhine, in what at that time was an entirely rural setting. In 1873 Clavel sold his works to a new company, "Bindschedler und Busch," Dr. Robert Bindschedler was a chemist, while Albert Busch was responsible for the business side.

The company grew rapidly. Within a decade, the workforce had increased from thirty to two hundred thirty. With the inevitable increase in capital requirements, there was growing pressure to transform the firm into a public limited company. This was duly completed on 19 December 1884 when the "Gesellschaft für chemische Industrie in Basel" was established with a capital stock of 2.5 million Swiss francs. The year 1884 is also regarded as the official "birthday" of the company. The abbreviation of its name, CIBA, is a protected trademark; it became so familiar that it was adopted as the official name of the company in 1945.

Before the turn of the century the range of dyestuffs was complemented by the first pharmaceutical products. As early as 1889 the company sent some of its drugs to the World Trade Exposition in Paris. Antipyrine, a fever remedy produced by CIBA, recorded huge sales during the great influenza epidemic of the following year. On the strength of this success, the pharmaceutical department was further expanded. The knowledge that infectious diseases are caused by microorganisms presented opportunities to combat the pathogens with chemical agents. One of the first successful pharmaceuticals to be marketed by CIBA was just such a bactericidal substance, Vioform, which was introduced in 1900 as an antiseptic for the treatment of wounds and burns. It was on the market for many decades and its active ingredient was later used as the basis for a series of broad-spectrum intestinal antiseptics, the first of which was launched commercially in 1934. Now superceded by products draw-

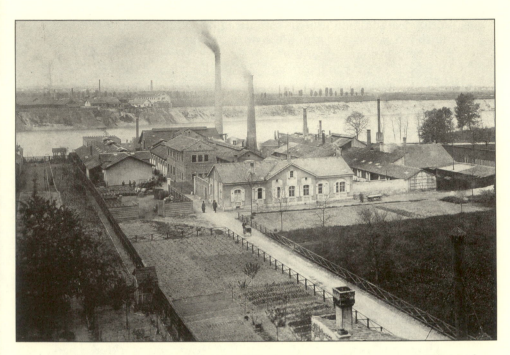

Chemical Comp. Bindschedler & Busch, 1879, the company later renamed CIBA Ltd.

ing on recent scientific advances, these antiseptics were for a long time the standard remedies in their category. This line of research also led CIBA into the field of tropical medicine with drugs active against schistosomiasis and leprosy. CIBA also developed sulfonamides. Launched shortly before the Second World War, Cibazol marked the beginning of a new era in the treatment of infectious diseases. As early as the beginning of the twenties, CIBA became particularly interested in the field of cardiovascular diseases. An early product of this research was the first synthetic cardiovascular agent Coramine, introduced in 1924. A turning point in the treatment of hypertension was signalled, in 1953, by the launch of Serpasil, the active ingredient of which stems from the root of the Rauwolfia plant, found in India. Further antihypertensive drugs followed, and also beta-blockers, which are used to treat cardiac arrhythmias and angina pectoris. Cardiovascular disease is still one of the three main areas in which Ciba-Geigy researchers are engaged.

CIBA also gained recognition in the field of hormonal therapy. Before the First World War, the company had launched various ovarian extracts onto the market. Scientific research into steroid hormones began in the early thirties. Elucidation of the structure of cholesterol opened the way for chemical processing. In rapid succession, the sex hormones were isolated, characterized and synthesized: in 1934, CIBA researchers succeeded in isolating progesterone; in 1935, the molecular structure of the male sex hormone testosterone was described, then partly synthesized; in 1948, the first partial synthesis of estrone, a product of the ovarian hormone estradiol, was accomplished. Numerous drugs, some of which are still in use today, resulted from these long years of research.

The first adrenal hormone product was launched by CIBA in 1939. A reaction developed by CIBA, which plays an important part in the extraction of cortisone from bile acid, linked the company with important developments in the area of corticoids. The sustained efforts in the field of corticosteroid research resulted in a series of antiinflammatory agents. A scientific breakthrough was achieved in 1961 with the total synthesis of the adrenocorticotropic hormone (ACTH or corticotropin), which is secreted by the pituitary gland and is responsible for regulating the function of the adrenal cortex. At that time, this polypeptide was the largest molecule to be synthesized and in the late 1960s was still the largest molecule in industrial production.

In 1960, CIBA acquired the Zyma Group, which has its headquarters in Nyon, in the canton of Vaud. The drugs produced by Zyma, primarily for treatment of diseases of the circulatory system, allergies, dermatitis, respiratory tract, and eye ailments, complemented the existing range of CIBA products.

From its traditional base in dyestuffs, fine chemicals and pharmaceuticals, CIBA diversified in the twenties, into cosmetics, plastics, and technical products. Pesticides followed after the end of the Second World War; later, products for veterinary medicine and hygiene. Finally, in the 1960s, the company diversified into electronic instruments and photochemical products. In 1970 it merged with J.R. Geigy Ltd.

Ciba-Geigy Ltd.

October 20, 1970, was a milestone in the history of the Basel chemical industry. On that day, eighteen months of negotiations between CIBA Ltd. and J.R. Geigy Ltd. were brought to a close when extraordinary general meetings of their shareholders approved the fusion of two companies that had followed separate historical paths, had many similarities, but still possessed quite different characteristics.

What led to the union between two such extraordinarily powerful partners? On several occasions since the turn of the century, the Basel dyes manufacturers had considered the possibility of merger. It was suggested as early as 1901 by a CIBA director. In 1916, a proposal to establish a joint plant for intermediate products was examined, but came to nothing. The first move in this direction came—as we have already mentioned—in 1918 when CIBA, Geigy, and Sandoz set up the Basler Interessengemeinschaft (IG), an agreement which, initially, was supposed to remain in force for fifty years. Although the combination soon became problematic because of the unforeseeably different evolutionary paths followed by the contracting partners, the benefits of the union should not be overlooked. Without it, the cartel negotiations with Germany, France, and Great Britain at the end of the twenties, which resulted in broad agreement among the companies operating in the international dyestuffs market, would probably not have been possible. It also had a decisive influence on the expansion of manufacturing facilities abroad, above all in Great Britain and the USA. During the Second World War, CIBA decided to place its majority holdings in IG joint ventures in England and the United States, and its shareholding rights in its own Canadian and U.S. subsidiaries, in the hands of an American trust. Geigy and Sandoz considered this to be in breach of the joint agreement and brought the case before a court of arbitration. At the end of 1950, following a hard-fought legal battle, the Basel interest group was prematurely dissolved.

During the next twenty years, all three companies were able to develop in a particularly favorable economic climate that was virtually untroubled by adversity of any kind. First signs of a shift in the relationship between CIBA and Geigy became apparent in the sixties. The main impulse was provided by the spectacular expansion of Geigy following its successes with DDT and crop protection agents. (It was another ten years before Ciba began systematic development of an agricultural chemicals sector.)

In 1967, Geigy overtook CIBA in terms of corporate sales, and the first ideas about future cooperation between the two companies were discussed. Initially, the discussion centered on a possible revival of joint activities in the dyestuffs sector. The foreign plants still run on a joint basis were an ideal platform from which to launch such a combination. Studies published in 1968 revealed that joint operations in this area would be of considerable benefit to both firms. Cooperation in the pharmaceuticals sector presented greater difficulties, particularly in view of the strict antitrust legislation and increasing state interference in the business activities of pharmaceutical companies. Opportunities for cooperation were also provided by spheres of activity which were well established at CIBA but represented fresh ground for Geigy, for example, plastics and photochemical products. Contacts were also established at the research level. A first and very important result of these talks was the establishment of a joint research center for biochemistry and medicine, the Friedrich Miescher Institute in Basel in 1969.

The potential benefits of a union became increasingly clear: lowering of overheads, elimination of overlaps on the production side, more muscle in the competitive field, and economies in capital expenditure and labor costs. Merger would pave the way for a more effective, concerted utilization of the available resources. At the beginning of 1969, the respective boards decided that the time had come to unite. During the year that followed, fusion—which had already been approved in principle—was delayed primarily by antitrust laws in the USA.

A detailed account of the intricacies of the merger is beyond the scope of this essay. But the form that was finally chosen for the fusion should be mentioned. Since the "equal status" of the two companies was undisputed, they eventually joined forces on a 1:1 basis. For fiscal reasons, a so-called "absorption fusion" was chosen as the official form of merger, i.e., J.R. Geigy Ltd. was taken over by CIBA Ltd. Thus, a group came into being which, today, twenty years on, is the world's seventh largest corporation in the chemical-pharmaceutical sector. Ciba-Geigy is active in pharmaceuticals, agrochemicals, plastics and additives, dyestuffs, chemicals, photochemical products, and electronic instruments. With more than 88,000 employees, the group generated sales totalling 17,647 million Swiss francs in 1988. The sales of the pharmaceutical division alone accounted for 5,168 million Swiss francs (30%).

Cardiovascular drugs, antirheumatics and other anti-inflammatory agents, psychotropic drugs, and anti-infectives are the mainstays of the product range, generating approximately three-quarters of sales. With Chiron Corporation, a company engaged in genetic engineering, Ciba-Geigy has established a joint venture in Emeryville, California. The object of the new enterprise is to develop and market synthetic vaccines. The research program aims at developing genetically engineered vaccines against diseases such as hepatitis, herpes, AIDS, and malaria.

Bibliography

Introduction:
Druey, Jean. *Forschungsergebnisse der schweizerischen pharmazeutischen Industrie.* Basel, 1973.
Forschung in Basel—Biotechnologie und Immunologie. Pharma Information: Basel, 1982.
Das Gesundheitswesen in der Schweiz. Pharma Information: Basel, 1987.
Jahresbericht 1988. Swiss Society for Chemical Industry: Zurich, 1989.
Koelner, Paul. *Aus der Frühzeit der chemischen Industrie Basels.* Basel, 1936.
Medikamente und pharmazeutische Industrie in der Schweiz. Swiss Society for the Chemical Industry: Zurich, 1987.
Pharma Daten Schweiz 1988. Pharma Information: Basel, 1989.

F. Hoffmann-La Roche & Co. Ltd:
Annual Reports
Fehr, Hans. *3 mal 25 Jahre: Fragmente aus der Roche-Geschichte.* Basel, 1967.
Der kleine La Roche. Basel, 1987.

Sandoz Ltd.:
Annual Reports
Corporate Archives
Riedl, Renate. *Alfred Kern und Edouard Sandoz, Gründer der Sandoz AG.*
Zurich, 1986.
75 Jahre Sandoz. Basel, 1961.

J. R. Geigy Ltd.:
Annual Reports
Bürgin, Alfred. *Geigy 1758–1939.* Basel, 1958.

CIBA Ltd.:
Annual Reports
Herkunft und Gestalt der Industriellen Chemie in Basel. Lausanne, 1959.

Ciba-Geigy Ltd.:
Annual Reports
Erni, Paul. *Die Basler Heirat. Geschichte der Fusion Ciba-Geigy.* Basel,
1979.

Universities, Industry, and the Rise of Biomedical Collaboration in America

by John P. Swann

INTERACTIONS between academe and the pharmaceutical industry are commonplace in America today. Exclusive, long-term, multi-million dollar research agreements between universities and firms abound—not just among the uppermost tier of research universities, but among dozens of academic institutions.[1] This paper will discuss how the foundation for this phenomenon emerged during the period between the two World Wars. The mind set of many American biomedical scientists in the early twentieth century included some formidable barriers to research interactions with commercial enterprises, which resulted in a highly tainted image of industrial work. Gradually this tainted image eroded, principally through the efforts of the pharmaceutical industry itself. Associations between academic scientists and drug companies grew closer, sometimes placing the university worker on intimate terms with a company's operations. Whether the academic researcher was a confidant of the company president or merely a grant recipient, the relationship often offered dividends to both sides. However, in the late nineteenth and early twentieth centuries, few academic scientists or pharmaceutical company presidents appeared to care what they might reap from joint research endeavors.

Growth of the Negative Image of Cooperative Research

Biomedical research, specifically fundamental research,[2] did not become a recognized function of universities in America until the last quarter of the nineteenth century. The intimate relationship between fundamental research and higher education was an innovation of German universities in the nineteenth century. This re-

Food and Drug Administration, History Office, HFC-24, Room 13–39, Rockville, MD 20857.

lationship spread to American universities as scientists and scholars returned from abroad, infected with the notion of *Wissenschaft* as a "dedicated, sanctified pursuit" of phenomena, "not the study of things for their immediate utilities, but the morally imperative study of things for themselves and for their ultimate meanings."[3] This concept of *Wissenschaft* as a search for ultimate meanings sprang from German idealism of the eighteenth and early nineteenth centuries, which had maintained close connections with universities through Kant (at Königsberg), Schelling (at Jena and Berlin), Hegel (at Berlin) and others.[4]

However, pure research was by no means the only pursuit of German academic researchers. The growing synthetic chemical industry in Germany developed close connections with several universities up to the 1880s, when many firms began concentrating on in-house research facilities. Companies provided university workers, from the institute director to the *Privatdozent*, with raw materials, consulting fees, patent royalties, and other means of support. In exchange, the academic chemists supplied industry with inventions, new production techniques, manpower in the form of graduates, and even expert testimony in the case of patent litigation. Eventually, the German chemical industry managed to help refashion the university chemical curriculum, in part to introduce the chemistry student to the needs of industry. As John Beer observed, firms developed especially close ties with several of the better academic laboratories:

Cooperation with university chemists was so actively sought by the various German companies that a veritable competitive struggle arose between them over the "control" of the most important academic laboratories; and in time each company managed to establish strong ties with certain schools to the exclusion of all other rivals. The Bayer firm had particularly close ties with [Wilhelm] Wislicenus at Würtzburg and with the University of Göttingen. Through the efforts of Carl Martius, the Agfa of Berlin had a virtual "monopoly" on [August Wilhelm von] Hofmann's findings and a first choice in the hiring of his students. Höchst and the Badische Anilin- und Soda-Fabrik competed, or sometimes cooperated, for the favor of Adolph Baeyer, who taught successively in Berlin, Strasbourg, and Munich, and of Baeyer's many gifted students, such as [Carl] Graebe, [Carl Theodor] Liebermann, Emil and Otto Fischer, and Ludwig Knorr.[5]

Clearly, such a situation was far removed from any sort of disinterested search for ultimate meanings or from the Veblenian cult of idle curiosity.

Thus, higher education in Germany wore two distinctly different masks. On one hand, the state governments kept the technical schools apart from the universities to use the former to promote industrialization. Also, about three quarters of the university lectureships (at least in chemistry) were devoted to "pure" fields throughout the last quarter of the nineteenth century.[6] However, the links between academe and industry obviously were close, which posed a confusing situation when the Americans arrived. Americans emigrated to German universities primarily in the 1870s, 1880s, and 1890s. Peak emigration came in 1895–1896, when over 500 Americans enrolled in German institutions. That study in Germany was cheaper (even when including the cost of travel) than study at some of the better universities in the United States played some part in a student's decision to spend time at a German university, but the intellectual challenge alone was overwhelmingly attractive for most.[7]

Several American universities—some new, such as Clark, Stanford, and Chicago, and some refurbished, such as Harvard, Yale, and Cornell—followed the lead of Johns Hopkins in 1876 by establishing graduate research programs based on the German model (without the ties to industry). By 1900 some state universities, including Wisconsin, California, and Michigan, established graduate research programs as well. Soon, the number of doctorates conferred by American universities increased dramatically, from zero in 1861 to 164 in 1890, and the postgraduate population in America rose from about 200 students in 1871 to nearly 3000 in 1890.[8]

Qualitatively, Americans brought back with them the fundamental component of the German research experience, which accelerated the extant attitudes in American scientific education about the value of original and basic research.[9] An early *Register* of Johns Hopkins proclaimed that the Baltimore university "provides advanced instruction, *not professional*, to properly qualified students, in various departments of literature and science."[10] Clark University was established in 1888 as a graduate school alone. Few American educators were as ardently supportive of fundamental research as psychologist G. Stanley Hall, the first President of Clark University. He likened research-oriented professors to prophets, freed from the "routine and rules of common college life," in an atmosphere devoid of the practical components of Francis Bacon's "House of Solomon": "In the new 'House of Solomon' they should have the best equipment, the largest pay, the freest air; for thus not merely the university, but the nation, receives with due honor its anointed prophets."[11]

But what of the other "industrialized" side of German higher education in the late nineteenth century, and its affect on the Americans? To assume that this even had an immediate effect presupposes that the visiting Americans had some involvement in the links with the firms, which is doubtful. Their purpose in leaving the States was to learn chemistry, or physiology, or pharmacology, not to find support for these fields. Yet, even if they had some exposure to the connections with firms, there was nothing in America to which such connections could be compared. Nineteenth-century American companies were by and large primitives in research. In fact, interactions between American companies and universities did not begin to approach the same level of sophistication and intensity that German academic-industrial ties exhibited until the period between the two World Wars.

Fundamental research played an incontestably important part in the development of the American university in the late nineteenth century, but the latter also had a well-established utilitarian component.[12] For example, the Morrill Land Grant Act of 1862, the Hatch Act of 1887 (which established agricultural experiment stations), and the second Morrill Act of 1890 (which helped subsidize the agricultural colleges established under the 1862 Act) provided for practical instruction in many universities. By the turn of the twentieth century, the American university emerged as an amalgam of fundamental and applied research functions:

In the one view, research was an activity to be initiated and directed from within the university. The searcher was to be independent, not only with respect to his conclusions, but to his choice of an area of work. To fill the gaps in knowledge that continuing inquiry revealed, to conduct investigations as the logic of a discipline directed—these were to be the functions of academic inquiry. Practical results might be forthcoming, but inquiry should be allowed to push against any of the frontiers of knowledge, and not merely along that border where material benefits were promised ... [But] the graduate school in the American university was only one of a heterogeneous group of divisions. In the other schools and departments [for example, agriculture, commerce, engineering, and business administration], research was often geared to external and ulterior purposes.[13]

Notwithstanding the presence of practical interests, the strength of fundamental research in universities probably played some part in the reluctance of biomedical researchers to collaborate with pharmaceutical companies. Many physiologists, biochemists, pharmacologists, and other biomedical scientists spent time in Germany in the late nineteenth and early twentieth centuries, including some of the most prominent workers in their fields. Pharmacologist John J. Abel of Johns Hopkins spent seven years in Germany; physiological chemist Russell Chittenden of Yale and physiologist Jacques Loeb (Loeb having spent nearly twenty years at Chicago and Berkeley before moving to the Rockefeller Institute) also brought German ideals of pure learning to America. These disciplines certainly faced practical obligations in settings such as medical and agricultural schools,[14] but such "service roles" did not lead to the abandonment of pure learning in the biomedical sciences. Chittenden, the father of American biochemistry, developed a successful compromise between purely theoretical work and practical instruction at the Sheffield Scientific School.[15] Abel, Chittenden's counterpart in pharmacology, believed that, once established, pharmacology would "yield valuable results for the practical man." He emphasized, however, that pharmacology "is not therefore an applied science, like therapeutics, but is one of the biological sciences, using that word in its widest sense."[16]

It was one thing for biomedical researchers to spend time training physicians and other professionals, but working with industry was an entirely different matter. Until the early twentieth century, American drug companies by and large had no interest in research. There were a few exceptions, such as H. K. Mulford and Parke-Davis, but even these firms had little or no interest in fundamental work. After research had become a recognized function for many pharmaceutical companies, Abel still refused to do any work for drug firms:

I personally would not think of working on a problem suggested to me by any firm anywhere. Usually, problems of this nature could be worked out very well in the laboratories of the firms since they almost always concern questions of what I might call applied pharmacology. A pharmacologist of any training or ability should have so many problems of his own awaiting solution that he should not spend his time on matters of little theoretical importance for his science.[17]

The high value placed on fundamental research in American universities, therefore, helped impede any movement for collaboration with pharmaceutical firms on strictly applied work. Traditional disapproval of medical patents by physicians and biomedical scientists also blocked cooperative work from within academe. The Code of Ethics that the American Medical Association adopted in 1847 explicitly decried medical patents.[18] Harvard bacteriologist Hans Zinsser proclaimed why physicians and medical researchers had such an aversion to medical patents:

The invention of an improvement in the mechanism of automobiles, or of a shoe-buckle, concerns matters of convenience or luxury, and can be dispensed with easily by those who are forced to do without them. The relief of the sick and the prevention of unnecessary sorrow by the maintenance of individual and public health are matters in a different category. As soon as we are in possession of the knowledge of principles or methods which can contribute to these purposes their free utilization becomes a public necessity; and any procedure which inhibits their most rapid and effective application to the needs of the community would seem to us as unjustified as the cornering of the wheat market or the patenting of the process of making bread.[19]

Abel, too, questioned the ethics of patenting medical discoveries: "I have always considered it unethical for a medical man, and especially for a research worker who is supported by a university and foundations, to take out patents."[20]

The American pharmaceutical industry did not make significant use of the patent system until after World War I. Rather, German drug companies held the vast majority of American patents on therapeutic agents. Several American firms received licenses to produce these patented drugs after the United States government abrogated German-owned patents under the Trading With the Enemy Act of

1917.[21] Before the war, drug companies protected their processes through secrecy;[22] the American Medical Association had long censured this means of protection as well as patenting.[23]

It may seem incongruous to conceive of an unwillingness within academe to cooperate with the pharmaceutical industry on the basis of anti-patent bias, given the actual paucity of patent activity by American firms. However, university scientists had no reason to doubt that American firms would turn to patents to protect their research investments—much like the German industry—once they established research programs.[24] To realize such programs, of course, required the cooperation of academic researchers. In a sense, drug companies in the late nineteenth and early twentieth centuries were damned if they did and damned if they did not. Academic scientists found it difficult to take firms seriously as potential collaborators until companies developed an interest in research. Yet, once firms established research programs of their own, they would in all likelihood (based on the experience of German firms) become more aggressively patent-minded. Ironically, academic biomedical scientists themselves began seeking patents in earnest in the 1920s and 1930s.

Given all of the above, it should not be surprising that academic scientists had a tainted image of industrial pharmaceutical work by the late 1910s. As one indication of this image, consider the reaction of scientists when Max Gottlieb—the creation of Sinclair Lewis and bacteriologist Paul De Kruif, based in part on Jacques Loeb—abandoned academic life to work for the fictional pharmaceutical firm, Dawson T. Hunziker and Co., Inc. Scientists lamented, " 'How could old Max have gone over to that damned pill-peddler?' " and " 'Of all the people in the world! I wouldn't have believed it! Max Gottlieb falling for those crooks. . . . I wish he hadn't gone wrong!' "[25] *Arrowsmith* was a novel, but the depiction of the alarm and dismay of his academic colleagues when a respected scientist joined a drug company reflected the opinion of many biomedical scientists and physicians about connections with industry. John Parascandola's paper in this volume discusses a nonfictional example of how one scientific society dealt with industrial biomedical scientists.

The Tainted Image Erodes

Several developments within the pharmaceutical industry between World War One and World War Two helped dissolve the academic biomedical community's disparaging view of this industry, and thereby opened the way for widespread cooperation between industry and academe. The most significant developments were: a major change in attitude among many firms, emphasizing the value of research and an active application of this philosophy (including the support of some fundamental research); employment of prominent scientists, often as directors of company research; and establishment of special research laboratories and research institutes.

The neglect of product development by American manufacturers became quite obvious during World War One when German firms interrupted drug supplies to the United States. German drug companies had introduced some of the leading analgesic, anesthetic, hypnotic, antimicrobial, and other agents, and they employed a variety of trade practices to maintain control of the markets for these drugs in the United States. As the war dragged òn these drugs became scarcer and prices skyrocketed. After the government abrogated German patents near the end of the war, American pharmaceutical firms soon filled the demand for these drugs, partly because many firms already had trained staff for control work, and partly because outside scientists assisted some firms. Essentially, this experience introduced many firms to the potential riches of product development.[26]

If American firms learned anything from their German counterparts after the war, they learned that to remain at the cutting edge of practical therapeutics research was essential. Thus Alfred S. Burdick, President of Abbott Laboratories, proclaimed, "Research is fundamental and vital. Without it real progress is impossible, in spite of occasional evanescent success."[27] According to Carlton Palmer, president of Squibb, his firm could not neglect in-house research:

We cannot afford to discontinue all research work even though we connect with the Mellon Institute and use their data to solve our bigger problems. Just whether we need any additional men or whether we do not possess men on our present staff sufficiently qualified to take charge of our research work I leave to you to decide. But I do feel that we should have a regular research department . . .[28]

Industry leader Josiah K. Lilly recognized the need for a solid foundation of chemists, pharmacologists, biologists, pharmacists, and clinicians "to insure a steady stream of useful and profitable specialties to Eli Lilly and Company."[29] From the time he assumed the chief executive position of Merck and Company in 1925, George Merck planned a research laboratory of the highest order, on a level equal to the best academic laboratories:

To do research worthy of the name, to do research which will bring to industry true recognition of its contribution to the advance of knowledge, industry must have at its disposal genuinely creative minds so placed and so protected that their mental powers of thought, study, and imagination can concentrate on problems of great difficulty.[30]

These and other pharmaceutical company executives put their strong convictions about research into action. Abbott, for example, was appropriating about $100,000 annually for research by the late

1920s, and it had a research and control staff of twenty-nine by 1933.[31] The Upjohn Company's research staff had grown to a similar size by this time.[32] Merck's research program grew slowly in the 1920s, but this changed in the next decade; from 1931 to 1940, Merck annual research expenditures ballooned from $146,000 to $906,000 (the latter sum was four percent of the company's total sales for 1940).[33] Squibb had only a handful of researchers at the end of World War One, but by 1928 the firm's research staff totalled at least fifteen (not including scientific personnel at its biologicals laboratory), with a research budget of about $200,000 each year.[34] Lilly, by the mid-1930s, had one of the largest research and control staffs in the industry. Its personnel in analytical, organic, and biochemistry; pharmacology; bacteriology and immunology; and other divisions amounted to over seventy, forty of whom held graduate or professional degrees.[35] Parke-Davis had built up such a research program that, in 1924, President Oscar W. Smith appointed a research committee, which included a physician, a Ph.D. in pharmacology, and a Ph.D. in organic chemistry.[36]

That company executives wanted to establish research programs is clear. That they really understood how to establish a research program was another matter. For example, Carleton Palmer of Squibb wanted his firm to have a research department, but he was not quite sure how or whether to add to his research staff. George Merck stood solidly behind research at his firm. When he would walk around the laboratories, talking to the bench scientists, "he would get all excited about what people were telling him. He didn't understand it, but you could see he was getting all excited about it."[37] This is not surprising, since Palmer, Merck, and many other executives in the drug industry between 1920 and 1940 were businessmen, not scientists. Thus they, and even executives with some scientific background like the Lillys and Alfred Burdick of Abbott, turned to outside scientists to create research departments.

John F. Anderson joined Squibb in 1915 as Director of the Research and Biological Laboratories. Twelve years earlier Anderson had been the first to identify Rocky Mountain spotted fever, and he suggested the wood tick (*Dermacentor andersoni*) as the probable vector. He had served in the United States Public Health Service since 1901, and he was the Director of the Service's Hygienic Laboratory from 1909 until the time he joined Squibb.[38] Ernest Volwiler joined Abbott as a research chemist the same year he graduated from Illinois, in 1918. Volwiler was named Chief Chemist in 1920, and he quickly assembled a string of impressive therapeutic discoveries, most notably in hypnotics and sedatives. He became Director of Research at Abbott in 1930.[39] George Henry Alexander Clowes studied chemistry in his native England and took a Ph.D. in that field at Göttingen before emigrating to the United States in 1901. His first position in the States was at the New York State

Institute for the Study of Malignant Disease in Buffalo, as a research chemist. Clowes soon developed an interest in cancer research, and became part of a small circle of pioneering researchers in that field. He worked in the Chemical Warfare Service and at the Marine Biological Laboratory at Woods Hole from 1917 to 1919, when he accepted the Lilly's offer to organize a research program in Indianapolis as Director of Research.[40]

Other firms soon followed suit. In 1920 Parke-Davis hired Oliver Kamm, an organic chemist on the faculty of the University of Illinois, as Director of Chemical Research. F. Hoffmann-La Roche and Company was in the process of establishing a research program at its New Jersey plant, independent of its parent firm in Switzerland, when it appointed physiologist Friedrich Gudernatsch (Ph.D., German University, Prague, 1910) as Director of Research Laboratories in 1929. Gudernatsch had spent several years prior to this appointment on the faculty of the Cornell Medical College; throughout his Directorship he was a visiting professor at New York University.[41] On the recommendation of Princeton physical chemist Hugh Taylor,[42] George Merck invited a rising organic chemist at Princeton, Randolph Major, to head research at his firm. Major joined Merck as Director of Pure Research in 1930. Sharp and Dohme engaged pharmacologist John Krantz of the University of Maryland School of Pharmacy briefly (1927–1930) as Director of Pharmaceutical Research. A long-time faculty member at Johns Hopkins Medical School, George Harrop, came to Squibb in 1937 as Director of the Squibb Institute for Medical Research.

In addition to these well-respected research directors, many bright young scientists came to work for pharmaceutical companies in the 1920s and 1930s. Among those hired were pharmacologist David Macht (beginning in 1925) at Hynson, Westcott, and Dunning; biochemist George Cartland (1927) at Upjohn; pharmacologist K. K. Chen (1929) and biochemist M. E. Krahl (1933) at Lilly; pharmacologist Harry van Dyke (1938) at Squibb; and chemists William Ruigh (1930), Karl Folkers (1934), Max Tishler (1937), and pharmacologist Hans Molitor (1932) at Merck.

Several leading, research-conscious companies established special research units in the 1930s, such as the Merck Research Laboratory, which included the Merck Institute for Therapeutic Research (founded in 1933), the Lilly Research Laboratories (1934), the Squibb Institute for Medical Research (1938), and the Abbott Research Laboratories (1938). Some companies, like Parke-Davis and Lilly, had established research laboratories as early as the first decade of this century. The difference was that the earlier laboratories only went so far as to establish a comparatively rudimentary level of science in the pharmaceutical industry, typically in the form of quality control work, whereas laboratories established in the 1930s contributed to the general stream of pharmacomedical sciences.

The research laboratories and institutes typically opened with much fanfare. Major scientists and others from universities, the federal government, and private research foundations addressed assemblies of prominent scientists and physicians at dedication ceremonies. The speakers at the Merck Research Laboratory dedication, for example, included Surgeon General Hugh S. Cumming, industrialist Lammot Du Pont, and British pharmacologist Henry Dale. Dale, Irving Langmuir of the General Electric Research Laboratory, pharmacologist Carl Voegtlin of the United States Public Health Service, Frederick Banting of insulin fame, and the discoverers of the value of liver in anemias, George Minot and George Whipple, were among the speakers at the dedication of the Lilly Research Laboratories.[43]

In their addresses to these distinguished audiences, the executives and research directors of these firms emphasized the high level of scientific research—even fundamental work—to be expected from these research units, the need for closer cooperation between universities and the drug industry, and the separate status of these research units with respect to the business interests of the firm. George Merck informed his audience in Rahway, New Jersey, that the Merck Research Laboratory was made up of an applied research department, the Merck Institute of Therapeutic Research, and a "Pure Research division" devoted "to the study and preparation of new chemicals of scientific interest." G. H. A. Clowes reminded the Lilly audience of his company's support of basic research:

... [J. K. Lilly] and Mr. Eli Lilly fully appreciated the value of fundamental research and were not only willing but eager and anxious that we should conduct investigations in certain fields in which there could be no possible hope of any commercial return. ... What question could there possibly be regarding association with an organization directed by men holding such an enlightened point of view?[44]

Abbott Research Director Ernest Volwiler touched on the need for closer cooperation between industry and universities: "Your presence here today to join in the dedication of this new research building shows your belief that new steps forward in hygiene must come about through the mutual efforts of the medical arts and all the accessory sciences; of the university and industry; of the individual worker in science and the highly organized group." J. K. Lilly recalled that many therapeutic agents—"adrenalin, tryparsamide, thyroxin, viosterol, insulin, liver extract, parathyroid extract, ephedrine"—all derived from collaborative work.[45] George Merck proclaimed that the Merck Institute operated as a foundation independent of Merck and Company, a proclamation that President Carleton Palmer echoed five years later in his dedication address at the Squibb Institute.[46]

All of the factors discussed in this section—the growing support of research in the pharmaceutical industry, the slow migration of prominent academic scientists to industry to organize and direct company research programs, the movement of promising young scientists into industrial positions, and the sudden emergence of a cluster of industrial research institutes and laboratories—helped break down the barriers to collaborative biomedical research between the two World Wars. Successful collaborations early in this period, such as the work between Roger Adams and Abbott on barbital and procaine and the introduction of insulin through the joint efforts of the University of Toronto and Lilly, fueled the movement for cooperative work. Alfred S. Burdick's address to the American Pharmaceutical Manufacturers' Association, in the early 1930s, testified to this change of venue in cooperative work:

> I also want to stress cooperation in research. There never was a time, for instance, when the university men were so eager to collaborate with commercial houses as they are now. I remember when we first started in, the average college professor working in the field was a haughty creature. He would not be tainted with commercialism in any form. His research was academic, for purposes of science. I may say that is all changed. They are just as eager to have friendly relations with commercial houses as any other type of men. In fact, they come to me almost every day or every few weeks— men connected with universities that are following certain lines of research, whose funds have run out or are not available on account of the present depression, eager and anxious to make commercial connections with people who will finance them. Some of these things have great promise. It would really be for the benefit of mankind if some of you men who have surplus funds, if any of you have and I hope you have, would consider some of these possibilities.[47]

The so-called "haughty creatures" of academe and pharmaceutical companies interacted more and more during the 1920s and 1930s. Companies typically supported research in universities at this time through fellowships or grants. These were payments made either to the professor to disburse as he saw fit or to a student working under that professor, in the form of a stipend. The specific terms of these awards varied from company to company and from fellowship to fellowship within each firm. Some fellowships were purely philanthropic, but by and large fellowships served immediately strategic purposes.[48] For example, the company might insist on choosing the research topic as a means to supplement or perhaps substitute for in-house research.[49] Also, the firm might make prior arrangements for the disposition of any discoveries made in the professor's laboratory. A firm often awarded a grant or fellowship simply to maintain an open channel of communication with a researcher at the forefront of a particular field.[50]

One way to estimate the growth of university-industry research interactions in this period is to examine the increase of fellowships. Research Information Service of the National Research Council published surveys of fellowships in science and technology in 1923,

1929, and 1934.[51] The data pertaining to academic fellowships sub-
sidized by pharmaceutical firms are summarized below.

Year	Companies	Fellowships	Total Amount
1923	4	8	$6,300
1929	6	19	$13,200
1934	10	40	$37,050

The surveys certainly suggest an increasing amount of interaction
between biomedical scientists in universities and the pharmaceutical industry. However, detailed investigations of selected firms suggest these data are considerably incomplete. Companies were not
always willing to divulge the names of the groups they were supporting for fear that competitors might get wind of their research
activities and interests. Some university workers, too, were reluctant
to publicize the fact that they were receiving support from a firm.
They felt their colleagues would look askance at any of their publications throwing a good light on a supporting firm's product.

From 1925 to 1930, Squibb's fellowship support increased significantly, as the firm's total research budget grew: 1925, $18,400;
1926, $15,900; 1927, $18,000; 1928, $22,400; 1929, $30,200; and
1930, $48,609. Overall, fellowships represented one-seventh of the
total research expenses for these years.[52] Thus, Squibb seems to have
relied on university laboratories as a significant additional source
of research. Upjohn instituted a major fellowship program in 1933.
The firm awarded a dozen fellowships each year, ranging from $1800
to $5000, and the fellows spent the year at Upjohn.[53]

Merck also invested a major sum in academic research fellowships
by the late 1930s. In 1939, that firm funded seventeen projects at
11 institutions for a total of $38,500. Unlike the case with Squibb
in the late 1920s, Merck's fellowships amounted to no more than
about five percent of its total research expenses.[54] Reliable information exists for selected years throughout this period for Lilly. In
1925, soon after its successful and widely publicized collaboration
with the University of Toronto on insulin, Lilly formed research
contacts with academic workers at eleven institutions.[55] Unfortunately, the amount of Lilly's support is unknown. Five years later,
following other major collaborations—with Harvard and with Roch-
ester on liver extracts for anemias—Lilly's fellowship activity grew.
The company established seventeen fellowships in fourteen universities, worth nearly $32,000.[56] By 1942 this sum increased to over
$87,000 annually, representing forty-five fellowships in twenty-seven
academic institutions—about eleven percent of the firm's total research expenditures.[57]

As seen by Merck, Squibb, Upjohn, and Lilly, industry and academe interacted more and more during this period. Also, scientists
began organizing themselves to promote or at least facilitate co-

operative research. For example, pharmaceutical scientists organized the National Conference on Pharmaceutical Research in 1922 to encourage and coordinate pharmaceutical research. Academic and industrial scientists served side-by-side on the Conference's Executive Committee and various scientific committees, which reviewed research of the previous year in medicinal chemistry, bacteriology and biologicals, pharmacology and bioassays, and other areas. The Conference lasted through the 1920s and 1930s.[58] Academic and industrial scientists also worked together on many committees for the United States Pharmacopeial Convention. Representatives from Squibb, Parke-Davis, and Mulford served with five university workers and one government scientist on the Subcommittee on Bioassays that was appointed for the 10th revision of the Pharmacopeia, beginning in 1920.[59] The National Research Council established a Committee on Chemical Research on Medicinal Substances to promote contacts between industry and academe. Among the members of this Committee were industrial researchers Frederick Heyl of Upjohn and Arthur Dox of Parke-Davis, and university chemists who were seasoned collaborators with the pharmaceutical industry, such as Roger Adams of Illinois, Frank Whitmore of Northwestern (and later Pennsylvania State), and Treat Johnson of Yale.[60] Thus, ample opportunities existed for the union of university researchers and pharmaceutical companies—opportunities generated from within academe as well as industry—by the dawn of World War Two.

Conclusion

Universities and pharmaceutical companies stood to gain considerably from cooperative research, yet they also ran certain risks to themselves and to the public health. The attraction of a source of funding led more than a few academic scientists to focus on industrial problems in which they otherwise had little or no interest. Also, the proprietary nature of the collaborative research certainly created some concern (which was justified in more than a few cases) that researchers might not share their research with colleagues through publications, student theses or dissertations, or informal dialogues at professional meetings. Collaboration had disadvantages for companies as well. Sharing proprietary information with outsiders ran a risk of intelligence leaks. Also, a firm possibly could damage the development of an in-house research program by relying too heavily on contracted research. From the standpoint of the public, university workers and companies often entered into exclusive arrangements, entitling the collaborating firm to a monopoly on any discoveries made by the academic researcher. Such arrangements threatened the economics of health care with their potential to inflate drug prices.

On the other hand, industrial support of medical and pharmaceutical research in universities grew at an important time. During the period between the wars, the massive support by private foundations (Rockefeller, Carnegie, Macy, etc) was slowly declining, particularly during the Depression, and the federal government had not yet begun to support research at high levels.[61] The contact with academe helped industry, too. First, universities offered companies their valuable experience in research, and second, no matter how far developed, an industrial laboratory alone could not possibly attend to all research needs in every field. Finally, between 1920 and 1940 collaborations between the two sides yielded important hormones (insulin); anticonvulsants (Dilantin); sedatives, hypnotics, and anesthetics, (Pentothal); chemotherapeutic agents (streptomycin); and several other drugs. Therapeutics and public health thus shared some of the benefits of cooperative research.

Notes and References

1. For example, see Martin Kenney, *Biotechnology: The University-Industrial Complex* (New Haven: Yale University Press, 1986), and Lois S. Peters and Herbert I. Fusfeld, "Current U.S. University/Industry Research Connections," in *University-Industry Research Connections: Selected Studies*, Report of the National Science Board of the National Science Foundation [Washington, D.C.: U.S.G.P.O., c. 1982].
2. By fundamental (or basic or pure research) I mean learning for its own sake, to supplement the sum understanding in a field without consideration of any other use. When I refer to applied (or practical) research, I mean learning for the sake of utility or public benefit other than pure intellectual elevation.
3. Richard Hofstadter and Walter P. Metzger, *The Development of Academic Freedom in the United States* (New York: Columbia University Press, 1955), 373.
4. Ibid., 370–372, and Joseph Ben-David and Awraham Zloczower, "Universities and Academic Systems in Modern Societies," *Arch. Europ. Sociol.* 3 (1962): 50–53.
5. John J. Beer, "Coal Tar Dye Manufacture and the Origins of the Modern Industrial Research Laboratory," *Isis* 49 (1958): 131 n. 24. See also Georg Meyer-Thurow, "The Industrialization of Invention: A Case Study from the German Chemical Industry," *Isis* 73 (1982): 365, 368, 376–377; Jeffrey A. Johnson, "Academic Chemistry in Imperial Germany," *Isis* 76 (1985): 506 ff.; and Timothy Lenoir, "A Magic Bullet: Research for Profit and the Growth of Knowledge in Germany around 1900," *Minerva* 26 (1988): 66–88.
6. Johnson, "Academic Chemistry," (n. 5), 513–514.
7. Laurence R. Veysey, *The Emergence of the American University* (Chicago: University of Chicago Press, 1965; Phoenix Books, 1970), 130, and Merle Curti, *The Growth of American Thought*, 3d ed. (New York: Harper and Row, 1964), 566.
8. Hofstadter and Metzger, *Development of Academic Freedom*, (n. 3), 377–379, and Curti, *Growth of American Thought*, (n. 7), 569.

9. Although fundamental research was not a recognized function of many American universities until the late nineteenth century, science courses certainly were common at American colleges by the 1820s; see Stanley M. Guralnick, "The American Scientist in Higher Education, 1820–1910," in *The Sciences in the American Context: New Perspectives*, ed. Nathan Reingold (Washington, D.C.: Smithsonian Institution Press, 1979), 99–141.

10. Quoted in Veysey, *Emergence of the American University*, (n. 7), 149.

11. G. Stanley Hall, "Research the Vital Spirit of Teaching," *Forum* (New York) 17 (1894): 561–562.

12. See Richard Harrison Shryock, "American Indifference to Basic Science during the Nineteenth Century," *Archives Internationale d'Histoire des Sciences*, no. 5, October 1948: 50–65, and Edmund Janes James' inaugural address as President of the University of Illinois, "The Function of the State University," *Science* 22 (1905): 609–628. Cf. Nathan Reingold, "American Indifference to Basic Research: A Reappraisal," in *Nineteenth-Century American Science: A Reappraisal*, ed. George H. Daniels (Evanston, IL: Northwestern University Press, 1972), 38–62, which argues persuasively against Shryock's thesis of the sudden emergence of basic research.

13. Hofstadter and Metzger, *Development of Academic Freedom*, (n. 3), 381–382.

14. For example, see Robert E. Kohler, *From Medical Chemistry to Biochemistry: The Making of a Biomedical Discipline* (Cambridge: Cambridge University Press, 1982); Gerald L. Geison, "Divided We Stand: Physiologists and Clinicians in the American Context," in *The Therapeutic Revolution: Essays in the Social History of American Medicine*, ed. Morris J. Vogel and Charles E. Rosenberg (Philadelphia: University of Pennsylvania Press, 1979), 67–90; and Russell C. Maulitz, " 'Physician Versus Bacteriologist': The Ideology of Science in Clinical Medicine," in ibid., 91–107.

15. Kohler, *From Medical Chemistry to Biochemistry*, (n. 14), 97–101.

16. John J. Abel, "The Methods of Pharmacology, with Experimental Illustrations," *Pharmaceutical Era* 7 (1892): 105.

17. J. J. Abel to W. deB. MacNider, 5 April 1935, John Jacob Abel Papers, Alan Mason Chesney Archives, Johns Hopkins University, Baltimore, Maryland (hereafter JA). For an example of an influential physical scientist's repudiation of commercial work, see Owen Hannaway, "The German Model of Chemical Education in America: Ira Remsen at Johns Hopkins (1876–1913)," *Ambix* 23 (1976): 145–164.

18. From *Code of Ethics of the American Medical Association*, chap. 2, art. 1, sec. 4, reproduced in Chauncey D. Leake, ed., *Percival's Medical Ethics* (Baltimore: Williams and Wilkins, 1927), 226.

19. Hans Zinsser, "Problems of the Bacteriologist in His Relations to Medicine and the Public Health," Presidential address delivered to the Society of American Bacteriologists, Philadelphia, 29 Dec. 1926, *Journal of Bacteriology* 13 (1927): 161.

20. J. J. Abel to S. L. Johnson, 21 September 1935, JA.

21. See Williams Haynes, *American Chemical Industry*, 6 vols. (New York: Van Nostrand, 1945–1954), 3: 481–508, 512–515.

22. Malcolm Keith Weikel, "Research as a Function of Pharmaceutical Industry: The American Formative Period," M.S. thesis, University of

Wisconsin, 1962, 56–57, and Jonathan Liebenau, *Medical Science and Medical Industry: The Formation of the American Pharmaceutical Industry* (Baltimore: Johns Hopkins University Press, 1987), 35.

23. *Code of Ethics of the American Medical Association*, chap. 2, art. 1, sec. 4, in Leake, *Percival's Medical Ethics*, (n. 18), 226.

24. This is precisely what Mulford did; see Liebenau, *Medical Science and Medical Industry*, (n. 22) 64.

25. Sinclair Lewis, *Arrowsmith* (New York: Harcourt Brace Jovanovich, 1925), 132; see also Charles E. Rosenberg, *No Other Gods: On Science and American Social Thought* (Baltimore: Johns Hopkins University Press, 1976), 123–131.

26. See, e.g., Liebenau, *Medical Science and Medical Industry*, (n. 22), 109–110, and Haynes, *American Chemical Industry*, (n. 21), 3: 311–326.

27. Quoted in Herman Kogan, *The Long White Line* (New York: Random House, 1963), 119.

28. C. H. Palmer to F. W. Nitardy [Plant Superintendent at Squibb], 30 March 1922, "M(1): Research and Development, General, 1920s," E. R. Squibb and Sons Archives, New Brunswick, NJ (hereafter ERS).

29. J. K. Lilly to E. Lilly and J. K. Lilly, Jr., 27 April 1926, "J. K. Lilly, Jr., Letters to and from Mr. Lilly, 18 February 1926–11 Sept. 1931," XCAc, Eli Lilly and Company Archives, Indianapolis, Indiana (hereafter ELC). See also Josiah K. Lilly, "Comments on Research in Manufacturing Pharmacy," in *Lilly Research Laboratories: Dedication* (Indianapolis: [Lilly,] 1934), 5–6, and Gene E. McCormick, "Josiah Kirby Lilly, Sr., the Man," *Pharmacy in History* 12 (1970): 64–65.

30. George W. Merck, "An Essential Partnership: The Chemical Industry and Medicine," *Industrial and Engineering Chemistry* 27 (1935): 739 (quotation), and Max Tishler, interview by Leon Gortler and John A. Heitmann, Wesleyan University Library, 14 Nov. 1983, 28–29, transcript, Beckman Center for the History of Chemistry, Philadelphia, Pennsylvania.

31. Kogan, *Long White Line*, (n. 27), 120, and Elmer B. Vliet, "The Abbott Story," lecture delivered at the Research-Development-Control Dinner, Abbott Auditorium, [North Chicago, Illinois,] 16 March 1950, 15-page typescript, 12, "Abbott—History," Abbott Laboratories Archives, North Chicago, Illinois (hereafter AL).

32. Leonard Engel, *Medicine Makers of Kalamazoo* (New York: McGraw-Hill, 1961), 91.

33. Merck and Company, *The Merck Corporation: Annual Report, 1931*, and "Merck and Co., Inc. and Consolidated Domestic Subsidiaries: Analysis of Research and Development Expenses," one-page typescript, 15 Nov. 1951, box 29, "Budget, 1953," Alfred Newton Richards Papers, University of Pennsylvania Archives, Philadelphia (hereafter AR).

34. F. W. Nitardy, "Research and Library Work," 7-page typescript (unpaginated), 24 March 1931, 6, ERS, and E. R. Squibb and Sons, "Annual Report," typescript, 8 April 1931, 49, "Research, 1900–1925," ERS.

35. Lilly, *Lilly Research Laboratories: Dedication*, (n. 29), 118.

36. O. W. Smith to [E. M.] Houghton, 5 February 1924, historical file, Parke-Davis Research Library, Ann Arbor, Michigan (copy in C(38)a, Kremers Reference Files, F. B. Power Pharmaceutical Library, University of Wisconsin, Madison, Wisconsin.

37. Tishler, interview by Gortler and Heitmann, (n. 30), 29.
38. Francis C. Wood, "John F. Anderson, 1871–1958," *Transactions of the Association of American Physicians* 72 (1959): 13–14, and "Dr. John F. Anderson, 1871–1958," *Squibb Sales Bulletin* [34] (1958): 541–542.
39. "Testimonial Dinner Tendered by His Friends and Associates in the Scientific Divisions to Dr. Ernest H. Volwiler in Appreciation of His Notable Services to Abbott Laboratories, to Science, and to Mankind since May 1, 1918," [Chicago] 26 March 1959, mimeograph, AL.
40. George H. A. Clowes, Jr., "George Henry Alexander Clowes, Ph.D., D.Sc., LL.D. (1877–1958): A Man of Science for All Seasons," *J. Surg. Onc.* 18 (1981): 197–217, and M. E. Krahl, "Obituary: George Henry Alexander Clowes, 1877–1958," *Cancer Research* 19 (1959): 334–336.
41. *American Men of Science*, 8th ed., s.v. "Gudernatsch, Dr. Friedrich."
42. Tishler, interview by Gortler and Heitmann, (n. 30), 28–29.
43. "Merck Research Laboratory Dedicated," *Merck's Report and Price List* 42 (1933): 82–85, and Lilly, *Lilly Research Laboratories: Dedication*, (n. 29). See also *The Field and the Work of the Squibb Institute for Medical Research* 1, no. 1 (1938); "Squibb Institute for Medical Research Dedicated October 11," *Squibb Sales Bull.* 14 (1938): 513–521; and *Addresses: Dedication of Research Building, Abbott Laboratories, North Chicago, Illinois, October 7, 1938* (North Chicago, Ill.: Abbott, 1938).
44. "Merck Research Laboratory Dedicated," (n. 43), 82, and G. H. A. Clowes, "Address by Dr. George H. A. Clowes," in *Lilly Research Laboratories: Dedication* (n. 29), 53–54.
45. Ernest H. Volwiler, "Introduction," in *Addresses: Dedication of Research Building, Abbott Laboratories*, (n. 43), 4, and Lilly, "Research in Manufacturing Pharmacy," (n. 29), 5. Note, however, that not all of the drugs that Lilly mentioned were products of collaboration between academic scientists and companies.
46. "Merck Research Laboratory Dedicated," (n. 43), 82, and Carleton Palmer, "Welcome," *The Field and the Work of the Squibb Institute for Medical Research* 1, no. 1 (1938): 3.
47. Alfred S. Burdick, "Research," address at the Annual Meeting of the American Pharmaceutical Manufacturers' Association, Greensboro, North Carolina, 18 May 1932, *Proceedings of the American Pharmaceutical Manufacturing Association*, 1931–1932: 373–374.
48. The Lilly Fellowship for the Study of Chemistry at the Johns Hopkins University, for example, was a philanthropic fellowship. It awarded a $1000 stipend to an Indiana resident for study at the Baltimore university; see Callie Hull and Clarence J. West, "Fellowships and Scholarships for Advanced Work in Science and Technology," 2d ed., *Bulletin of the National Research Council*, no. 72 (1929): 62. One could argue, of course, that such publicized "philanthropic" fellowships had strategic value—improving a firm's image. However, in terms of a company's research interests, such a fellowship was of marginal relevance at most.
49. See, e.g., the J. K. Lilly Fellowship no. 28 and no. 29 at the Purdue University College of Pharmacy, and the Parke, Davis and Company Fellowships in the Department of Chemistry at the Iowa State College of Agriculture and Mechanic Arts, in Callie Hull and Clarence J. West, "Fellowships and Scholarships for Advanced Work in Science and Technology," 3d ed., *Bull. Nat. Res. Council*, no. 94 (1934): 67, 120.

50. See, e.g., Squibb General Superintendent F. W. Nitardy to P. M. Giesy, 28 August 1923, "M(1): Research and Development, General, 1920s," ERS: ". . . we might contribute to the expenses of people who would . . . in return [keep] us informed on what was going on and what new things were under investigation, so that if anything of particular interest to E. R. Squibb and Sons were under investigation, we would have first hand information on it and could get in touch with the investigator personally if the case should warrant it. This, as you will see, is just for the purpose of linking the House up in some sort of a direct form with all the medical research work that is done in public institutions."

51. Research Information Service, "Fellowships and Scholarships for Advanced Work in Science and Technology," *Bull. Nat. Res. Council*, no. 38 (1923); Hull and West, "Fellowships and Scholarships," 2d ed., (n. 48); and Hull and West, "Fellowships and Scholarships," 3d ed., (n. 49).

52. E. R. Squibb and Sons, "Annual Report," 8 April 1931, 51, "Research, 1900–1925," ERS. Squibb supported a fellowship at one (at least) private research institution, the Mellon Institute, which is included in the data, but the bulk of Squibb's fellowships went to academic workers.

53. Engel, *Medicine Makers of Kalamazoo*, (n. 32), 89–90.

54. J. H. Gage to A. N. Richards, 12 December 1938, box 31, "Merck and Co., 1930–1939," AR.

55. [J. K. Lilly,] "Eli Lilly and Company: A History," 75, ELC.

56. Ibid., 91–92.

57. Minutes of the meeting of the Research Committee, Eli Lilly and Company, 1 July 1942, "Research Committee, 1942," +XRDj, ELC, and "Outline of 1943 Research Plan," sec. 6, p. 1, "Research Plans, 1942–1944," +XRDj, ELC.

58. See *Proc. Nat. Conf. Pharm. Res.*, which began publication in 1928, and the *Ann. Surv. Res. Pharm.*, which replaced the Conference's *Proceedings* and continued to be published until 1940.

59. Peter Stechl, "Biological Standardization of Drugs before 1928," Ph.D. diss., University of Wisconsin, 1969, 223–229. Industry scientists had played a prominent role in a similar committee, the Committee on Physiological Testing of the Scientific Section of the American Pharmaceutical Association, since its inception in 1910; see M. G. Allmark et al., "A History of the Committee on Physiological Testing, Scientific Section, American Pharmaceutical Association," *Drug Standards* 24 (1956): 200–205.

60. Haynes, *American Chemical Industry*, (n. 21), 4: 251–252.

61. Richard Harrison, *Past and Present* (New York: Commonwealth Fund, 1947); Shryock, *American Medical Research*, 88–174; George Rosen, "Patterns of Health Research in the United States, 1900–1960," *Bulletin of the History of Medicine* 39 (1965): 211–216; and Roger L. Geiger, *To Advance Knowledge: The Growth of American Research Universities, 1900–1940* New York: Oxford University Press, 1986):176, 191, 246–255.

The Early History of the Wellcome Research Laboratories, 1894–1914[1]

by E. M. Tansey and Rosemary C. E. Milligan

Hᴵˢᵀᴼᴿᴵᴬᴺˢ of British industry have identified the 1890s as a decade when "research within the firm" grew, a phenomenon that occurred in a climate of concern about the low level of scientific and technical education in Britain, especially when compared with Germany.[2] Industrial entrepreneurs were criticized, both by contemporary observers and later historians, for their concern with improving their social status instead of promoting industrial development and research.[3] Two notable exceptions to this charge were Ludwig Mond and Henry Wellcome, and this paper gives a broad outline of the first research laboratories associated with the latter's pharmaceutical company from the 1890s until the beginning of the first World War.

Burroughs, Wellcome & Co. and Early Research

Burroughs, Wellcome & Co.[4] was one of the first pharmaceutical firms to exploit and advertise new advances and technologies, such as the compressed tablets they marketed under the tradename "Tabloid." The firm had been founded in London in 1880 by two American pharmacists, Silas Mainville Burroughs and Henry Solomon Wellcome.[5] In response to increasing demand for their products the partners found it necessary to move to a larger site in Dartford six years after establishing manufacturing premises in south London (1883).

Both Burroughs and Wellcome insisted on the high and consistent quality of their preparations. A laboratory of some kind appears to have been included at the Dartford site, but this was almost certainly directly associated with manufacturing rather than research. How-

The Wellcome Foundation Ltd. and the Wellcome Institute for the History of Medicine, both at 183 Euston Road, London NW1 2BP, U.K.

ever, it is worth remembering "that what one man may describe as a 'research laboratory' another may, with apparently equal authority, call a development department. Who is to say, when we are dealing with organizations of eighty or more years ago, which description is correct?"[6]

As early as January 1891, an "experimental laboratory" was established on the third floor of the firm's commercial headquarters at Snow Hill in the City of London, although its function is not clear. At the same time, the Dartford factory included a "main pharmaceutical laboratory" and a " 'Kepler' laboratory," both concerned with manufacturing processes, and "a research laboratory," which probably analyzed their own and competitors products, and also developed chemical processes that could be transferred into the main production laboratories.[7]

In 1894 a significant development occurred—facilities were provided in central London for producing the new therapeutic agent diphtheria antitoxin. This was the beginning of what became the Wellcome Physiological Research Laboratories (WPRL), often claimed as the first of Henry Wellcome's "private" research laboratories.[8] The assumptions that Burroughs was not involved in the venture and that the establishment was also independent of the commercial firm must however be questioned.

The association between Burroughs and Wellcome seems to have been fraught with tension almost from the beginning of their partnership. Burroughs, the senior partner, tried to dissolve the partnership in 1888, unsuccessfully. The partnership was due for renewal in 1895, and by 1894 negotiations were again under way to sever it prematurely.[9] Thus, it was within this context of deteriorating personal and professional relations that the anti-toxin production was started. Since Wellcome was particularly careful to maintain a strictly legal business relationship with his partner, it is unlikely that Burroughs was not consulted about the new laboratory, although we have found no direct evidence of his involvement.

We must also question the frequent assertion made by Wellcome and his staff, that the WPRL, the Wellcome Chemical Research Laboratories (WCRL, established 1896), and his later laboratories and medical museums were all independent entities, clearly distinct from the commercial activities of the business. As will become apparent throughout this paper there were many close, profitable links between the separate parts of the Wellcome organization.

The "Physiological Research Laboratories," 1894–1899

The production of diphtheria antitoxin by Behring and Kitasato in 1890, and subsequent developments, stimulated research and development in many European and American laboratories. In 1894, Burroughs, Wellcome and Co. were one of the earliest suppliers in

Britain, their antitoxin being produced at premises in central London, "under the personal superintendence of an experienced London bacteriologist," now identified as T. J. Bokenham.[10] In 1896, *The Lancet* reported on the diphtheria antitoxins of nine institutions or companies, including three British producers: the British Institute for Preventive Medicine; Burroughs, Wellcome & Co., and the Leicester Bacteriological Institute.[11] All were criticized for providing antitoxins well below the claimed strength. During the subsequent enquiry at Burroughs, Wellcome & Co., Wellcome sought advice from outside experts, and Bokenham was ultimately replaced.

Bokenham's successor, Walter Dowson, was formally appointed Director in October 1897, indicating that the WPRL were now regarded as a separate entity requiring a Director. Under Dowson the antitoxin production flourished, and Wellcome started looking for a site where the laboratory could expand further. In late 1898, Brockwell Hall in Herne Hill, South London was identified as suitable for conversion into laboratories "carried out at very great expense, and no pains, labour, or money have been spared."[12] Despite occasional internal references to the "Wellcome Physiological Research Laboratories" in correspondence and memoranda this was not an official, consistent title until the laboratories moved to these new premises in Spring 1899.

The Wellcome Physiological Research Laboratories and the Home Office 1900–1901

An official report of the opening of the Laboratories described the extensive modern equipment and facilities available to the staff: a suite devoted to serum production, including incubation, culture, and packing rooms, and stables for the horses; substantial provision was made for bacteriological, chemical, and physiological researches, and a wide array of ancillary services were provided.[13] Such fittings provide a clue to Wellcome's intentions: he had realized that extensive animal experimentation was now necessary at the WPRL. First, the antitoxins had to be tested and quantified on small rodents, which was done by his staff on other premises for legal reasons explained below.[14] Second, drugs produced from animals, like extracts of suprarenal glands, could only be biologically tested, as there were no appropriate chemical tests of their purity.[15] Finally, Wellcome thought manufacturers like himself should encourage the performance of high quality research not connected to the commercial interests of the firm.

In Britain animal experimentation was subject to the constraints of the 1876 Cruelty to Animals Act (39 & 40, Vict.c.77). This law required individual researchers to be licensed by the Home Secretary on the recommendation of eminent scientific persons, with

The Wellcome Physiological Research Laboratories, Brockwell Hall,
Herne Hill, London, 1899–1922. From the Wellcome Institute Library,
reproduced by courtesy of the Wellcome Foundation Ltd.

additional certificates for specified experiments being granted by the
same procedure. All work had to be done on premises registered by
the Home Office. Thus, to perform the range of experimental work
he now envisaged, Wellcome needed the WPRL to be registered,
and he applied for the necessary authority in February 1900. This
application, the first by a commercial manufacturer, initiated a vast
debate within the Home Office and the medical profession.[16] Ironically, Wellcome, a successful business man anxious to promote and
support scientific endeavors, was handicapped by legislation and by
prevailing attitudes to commerce and trade. Such prejudices were
particularly obvious in the responses of some members of the Royal
Colleges of Physicians and Surgeons,[17] who resented any implication
that privileges accorded to them as men of science should also be
allowed to a mere "tradesman." The arguments, discussions, and
negotiations about Wellcome's application continued for eighteen
months. During this time Wellcome's employees who were licensees
had to perform the necessary standardization work on registered
premises elsewhere. Eventually, in September 1901, after a sustained
campaign, the laboratories were registered by the Home Office as a
place where experiments on living animals could be performed.[18]
Thus the WPRL was poised to develop a broad pharmacological
research program and was also able to offer, in collaboration with

the WCRL and the laboratories at Burroughs, Wellcome & Co., unique facilities for the testing and identification of newly developed or isolated pharmaceutical compounds.

The Wellcome Physiological Research Laboratories, 1901–1914

Home Office registration enabled Wellcome to employ physiologists and pharmacologists to perform "pure" research. In 1902 he directed that "To be quite consistent in all matters *re.* the Chemical & Physiological research laboratories being separate & distinct—we ought in all matters as far as practicable put this into effect."[19] Yet external prejudice against, and internal conflict about the laboratories continued, although professional restrictions such as the "preposterous provision" of the American Society for Pharmacology and Experimental Therapeutics excluding commercial pharmacologists[20] do not seem to have applied to Wellcome staff in Britain. However, the Pharmaceutical Society was publicly castigated in 1900 for not electing the Director of the WCRL, Dr. Power (see below), to its Fellowship,[21] and there was a hint in 1906 that the Physiological Society had blackballed a candidate from the WPRL "on the grounds of his supposed connexion with commercial interests." Corroborative evidence of this claim has not been found.[22]

Open distrust of the venture was still evident in 1904 when Henry Dale joined the WPRL, cautioned by his friends against association with a manufacturer. Dale himself "never had serious or lasting reason to regret the change" he had made, and his subsequent promotion to Director in 1906, on Dowson's resignation, determined the scientific direction and status of the WPRL.[23]

Home Office registration of the WPRL also increased the possibilities for collaboration between the different research components of Wellcome's empire. This was to some extent initiated by Dowson, who, in 1904, suggested to Wellcome: "I particularly desire to raise the question of the relation between the physiological laboratories and the Works at our next interview. It seems to me that this relation might with advantage to all concerned be more direct than it is at present."[24] From 1905 onwards, joint publications from the WPRL, the WCRL, and the Works were a common feature, probably owing much to the industry of Henry Dale. In February 1905 Walter Dowson wrote to Wellcome, "You are quite right about our physiologist but . . . so was I. His energies are all in the right direction. . . . Previously Dr. Barger [a chemist] could not get his things tested. Now with such a brilliant operator as Dr. Dale to help him, he cannot get out things fast enough for the physiological lab[ty]."[25] Wellcome annotated this with: "How about Dr. Power's products of research to keep him busy."[26]

However, the *independent* role of the WPRL, particularly in pure physiological research must also be emphasized. Some indication

Chemical research laboratory of the WPRL, photographed in November 1909. The figure at the bench is probably A. J. Ewins. From the Wellcome Institute Library, reproduced by courtesy of the Wellcome Foundation Ltd.

of the quality of the research work undertaken is that of the early employees at Brockwell Hall (1899-1914), nine ultimately became Fellows of the Royal Society, and two of these, Henry Dale, and A. T. Glenny achieved the distinction while employed by Wellcome.[27]

That independence was sometimes achieved after difficult negotiations. An awkward issue was raised in 1906, when Dale prepared a paper on his research on ergot of rye and adrenaline (epinephrine) for publication in *The Journal of Physiology*. When it came to publication, Wellcome objected to Dale using the word "adrenalin," since it was a registered trademark of a rival firm, Parke-Davis.

An experiment in progress in the experimental pharmacology laboratory of the WPRL, photographed in November 1909. The figure second from the left is probably Henry Dale. From the Wellcome Institute Library, reproduced by courtesy of the Wellcome Foundation Ltd.

Wellcome was particularly sensitive on the subject of trademarks as he protected his own, especially "Tabloid," with extreme vigilance. On the subject of adrenaline, Dale maintained, equally rightly, that within the British scientific community the word was used to denote the physiologically active principle of the adrenal glands. Within six weeks, at least forty letters and memoranda were exchanged between Wellcome, Dale, Dowson, and Power of the WCRL. Also drawn into the debate was J. N. Langley, Professor of Physiology at Cambridge, who gave authoritative support to Dale. Faced with such testimony, Wellcome permitted Dale to use the disputed word.[28]

By 1910, Henry Dale could write easily of the relationship between the WPRL and the company:

In addition to the drugs which have thus been investigated from all points of view in the Wellcome Physiological Research Laboratories, many others have there been physiologically examined which owe their production or chemical investigation to the Wellcome Chemical Research Laboratories or the experimental department of the Burroughs Wellcome Chemical Works. Incidental to this pharmacological work has been research on the purely physiological problems which it suggests and involves. Methods have also been originated and developed for controlling and standardising by physiological experiment the activity of those potent drugs to which chemical methods of assay are not appropriate.

Whilst devoted primarily to original research, the results of which appear from time to time through the ordinary channels of scientific publication, the laboratories have, therefore, also performed much work of a nature more directly applicable to the needs of Mr. Wellcome's firm.[29]

A similar, but often closer synergistic relationship had grown between the Wellcome Chemical Research Laboratories and the Company. To consider this development we must return to the 1890s.

The Wellcome Chemical Research Laboratories, 1896–1914

If Burroughs was involved, at least tacitly, in the decision to produce diphtheria antitoxins, he was clearly not associated with the creation of the Wellcome Chemical Research Laboratories. In December 1894, in the midst of the negotiations to dissolve the partnership, Burroughs fell ill and despite a temporary rally, died on 6 February 1895. Henry Wellcome thus became sole owner of the pharmaceutical company and he lost little time in establishing chemical research laboratories, clearly separate from the firm. Just eight days after his partner's death he wrote to his old college contemporary in America, Dr. Frederick Belding Power, telling him the sad news of Burroughs' death and adding:

Now Fred by the rule of fates I have become sole proprietor of this great business into which I have put my heart and the best years of my life. . . . My first thought is to desire you to come to London. I feel that I could aid you in your progress and I know that you can greatly aid me. What I suggest is that you come and let me fit up for you a most thorough and complete experimental laboratory near my offices, . . . I want you for constant consultation as I propose to enter much more into scientific medical chemical products. . . . I should not ask you to take up any business cares or actual manufacturing drudgery but only experimental and strictly scientific work etc such as I know is most congenial to you.[30]

Power had been Wellcome's close friend at the Philadelphia College of Pharmacy, graduating with him in 1874 and winning the College prize for Chemistry. He took his doctorate at Strassbourg University and then returned to the United States and established his reputation as an analytical chemist while heading the pharmacy department of the University of Wisconsin.[31] He eagerly accepted Wellcome's offer and the opening of the "Wellcome Research Laboratories" was celebrated on 21 July 1896 at a dinner in London.[32] The title used for the new laboratories is further evidence that at this date the Wellcome *Physiological* Research Laboratories had not been established as such.[33] Wellcome declared that these special laboratories were to be quite distinct from all his business departments

Dr. Frederick Belding Power, Director of the Wellcome Chemical Research Laboratories, 1896–1914. From the Wellcome Institute Library, reproduced by courtesy of the Wellcome Foundation Ltd.

and he hoped that something would be achieved of value to the world at large, "work carried out on no selfish lines . . . controlled and dictated with the highest regard for science."[34]

It was further announced that Power was to be joined by Dr. H. A. D. Jowett who had been chief assistant to Professor W. R. Dunstan at the Pharmaceutical Society's research laboratory. Together Power and Jowett established a laboratory on the third floor of a building near the headquarters of Burroughs Wellcome. In April 1898, on the appointment of Dr. S. B. Schryver, the fourth floor of this building was also converted to a laboratory but these soon became inadequate. On 24 May 1899, almost simultaneous with the move of the WPRL from Central London to Herne Hill, they transferred to 6 King St., Snow Hill, "a handsome modern building of Venetian style and architecture," and it was at this point that the laboratories became known as the "Wellcome *Chemical* Research Laboratories."[35] The ground floor contained the Director's office and a library holding, in addition to the usual publications, "a cabinet of the various substances prepared in the course of laboratory investigations, which [by 1900] already form[ed] a collection of considerable interest."[36] The laboratories proper were on the upper three floors, all provided with gas, electricity, telephones, and the most sophisticated equipment available for chemical analysis. This building was to serve them until the completion of the Wellcome Research Institution in 1932.

After moving to these new laboratories, the scientific staff increased and just over twenty men were employed between 1896 and 1914. In that time they published almost 170 papers,[37] the major work being "the complete chemical examination of a large number of plants or plant products which, on account of reputed medicinal value or other properties have been considered of special interest."[38] This somewhat traditional approach was in marked contrast to the innovative research being carried out in the WPRL, but if the chemistry was traditional, the laboratories were at least eager to investigate the properties of plants from all over the world. Power and his colleagues investigated over fifty different plants but his major contribution was on the chaulmoogra plant from Burma from which he isolated "chaulmoogric" and "hydnocarpic" acids. Within a few years Burroughs Wellcome was producing "Moogrol," one of the first of a series of leprosy treatments issued by the company. At the time of his death it was noted that on Power's researches "the whole of the modern treatment of leprosy is based."[39] This type of meticulous analysis enabled the isolation and production of several new substances. According to the 1914 report of WCRL, "In synthetic chemistry a number of new organic compounds have been produced and amongst inorganic salts several have been brought into new forms of combination whereby they have been rendered more suit-

The third floor laboratory of the WCRL, King Street, Snow Hill, London, 1899–1932. From the Wellcome Institute Library, reproduced by courtesy of the Wellcome Foundation Ltd.

able for medicinal use."[40] Having isolated these chemicals, the chemical and physiological laboratories then collaborated in their pharmacological testing.

The Connections Between the Research Laboratories and the Pharmaceutical Company

Despite the claim that the research laboratories were clearly independent from the firm, they did in fact serve Wellcome's commercial purposes and contributed greatly to his business success. The chemical laboratories seem to have had an easier relationship with the firm than did the physiological laboratories, perhaps because they were close physical neighbors in the City of London, and perhaps because Power was an old and valued friend of Wellcome.

The WCRL produced "Wellcome" brand fine chemicals, after an initial period when manufacture was carried out at the company's Dartford works by staff who had worked out the necessary processes at the WCRL. However, in 1898 a separate Chemical Department was created at Dartford headed by Dr. F. H. Carr, like Jowett, a protégé of Professor Dunstan. Processes initiated at the research laboratories were then transferred to the Chemical Department for development of large scale manufacturing. The Analytical Department of the Works, established in February 1897, ensured product purity.[41]

In 1905 a new Experimental Department was set up at the Works to establish and improve existing processes. This enabled the *Laboratories* to be devoted to more purely academic work and the *Chemical Department* to concentrate on manufacturing work proper. The first head of the experimental department was Dr. Jowett from the WCRL and a year later he became Manager of the Works, where he remained until he died, shortly after Wellcome, in 1936. Jowett was the first of many to transfer between the laboratories and the manufacturing works, and it was largely through his influence that staff at the Wellcome Chemical Works were also able to do research and publish on academic subjects, often in collaboration with their colleagues from both the Physiological and Chemical laboratories.

The Laboratories' Contribution to the Business

Thus the independence of Wellcome's laboratories from the firm was strongly proclaimed, but his business would not have progressed as it did without them. The contribution of the WCRL is illustrated by the price lists of "Wellcome" Brand Chemicals and Galenicals (published separately from the main Burroughs Wellcome Price Lists). By 1912,[42] the list encompassed over 160 items including several preparations pharmacologically validated by the WPRL. The "Wellcome" Brand Sera and Vaccines prepared at the WPRL "under the immediate supervision of a skilled staff of highly qualified experts," covered four pages of the Company's 1913 Price List.[43] They included not only the diphtheria antitoxins with which the laboratories originated, but also sixteen other antitoxins and seventeen vaccines against diseases such as cholera, influenza, and typhoid. The distinction between the laboratories and the company was maintained by the statement that Burroughs Wellcome & Co. merely acted as "distributing agents," but the commercial contributions of the laboratories to Wellcome's business is clear.[44]

The End of the Period

The years 1913/1914 were a watershed in the history of the Wellcome research laboratories, and not only because of the War. Since 1902, Wellcome had funded tropical research laboratories in Khartoum, and the idea developed of establishing in London an institution for the study of tropical medicine and hygiene. When the head of the Khartoum laboratories, Dr. Andrew Balfour, announced his intention of returning to England in 1913, Wellcome invited him to set up The Wellcome Bureau of Scientific Research in London. Balfour was to be not only Director of this Bureau but to have "the general control of the research work of the WCRL and the WPRL—

though such institutions may continue to be conducted separately under the present Directors or their successors—also of any other Research Laboratories, either at home or abroad, I may found."[45]

It is perhaps not wholly surprising that within eighteen months of Balfour's appointment, the directors of both existing laboratories had resigned. Henry Dale left the WPRL in June 1914 with his colleagues Barger and Ewins to join the newly created Medical Research Committee.[46] Power resigned from the WCRL in November 1914 "for family reasons" and returned to America.[47] He was replaced by Dr. F. L. Pyman, head of the Experimental Department at the Works since 1906. It was largely through his work that the WCRL was able in the early years of the war to produce "Kharsivan," a replacement for the German antisyphilitic compound Salvarsan. While the WCRL worked out ways of producing such German chemical products including aspirin, the WPRL produced massive amounts of antitoxins in response to military demands. At one period during the war more than 500 horses for antitoxin production were stabled at Brockwell Hall.[48]

In 1913 the Wellcome Bureau of Scientific Research was established as the first step toward unifying all Wellcome's scientific research work. This was furthered, in 1924, by the establishment of The Wellcome Foundation Ltd., which formally drew together for the first time the Burroughs Wellcome company, its overseas subsidiaries and the "independent" research laboratories and museums that Wellcome had created. In November 1931 the foundation stone was laid (in the Euston Road) for the Wellcome Research Institution,[49] the culmination of Wellcome's research plans started almost forty years earlier. This institution, it was announced, would house the Chemical Research Laboratories, the Bureau of Scientific Research, and the Historical Medical Museum. The Physiological laboratories remained at Beckenham where they had been located since 1922. Once again the separation of Wellcome's research institutions from his commercial company was stressed, perhaps for the last time.

It seems almost inconceivable now that the Research Laboratories are fully part of the business, that Wellcome truly believed that the laboratory work was noncommercial. However, on his death in 1936, Sir Henry Wellcome (knighted in 1932 and much honored for his services to science) willed The Wellcome Foundation Ltd. and all its constituent parts to the Wellcome Trust, a panel of five trustees who were to use the profits provided by the Company for the furtherance of medical and allied research.[50] For some time it was thought possible that the laboratories might be separated from the company and administered by the Trust.[51] It was finally realized that, despite Wellcome's intentions and his protestations to the contrary, the laboratories were an integral part of the business, which would be unable to function without them. Since then, the successors to the early laboratories established by Wellcome have developed the products on which the Company's profits, and hence the Trust's charitable funds, have depended. Thus they have been enabled, if indirectly, to fulfill the noncommercial ideals their founder espoused.

Notes and References

1. Material from the Archives of the Wellcome Institute (henceforward WI) is quoted with permission of the Trustees of the Wellcome Trust; that from the Archives of The Wellcome Foundation Ltd. (WF) is quoted with permission of The Wellcome Foundation Ltd. We thank Mr. J. D. Davies, Company Records Manager, and Mrs. M. F. Williamson, Assistant Archivist, for their help with WF papers. E. M. T. thanks the Wellcome Trust for financial support.

2. M. Sanderson, *The Universities and British Industry 1850–1970* (London, 1972), 20.

3. One suggestion is that English manufacturers only wanted to make enough money to enable them to stop manufacturing. H. J. Habbakuk, *American and British Technology in the Nineteenth Century* (Cambridge, 1962), 177.

4. The standard company history is G. Macdonald, *In Pursuit of Excellence* (London, 1980), *passim*, esp. 12–13.

5. For Burroughs see Macdonald, *In Pursuit of Excellence* (n.4), 19–21; and obituaries, e.g. *Chemist and Druggist* (16 February 1895): 254–258; *Pharmaceutical Era* (6 June 1895): 720–722. For Wellcome see C. M. Wenyon, "Sir Henry Solomon Wellcome," *Obituary Notices of Fellows of the Royal Society* 2 (1938): 229–238; *Sir Henry Wellcome, a Biographical Memoir* (London, 1953); H. Turner, *Henry Wellcome, the Man, his Collections and his Legacy* (London, 1980); R. C. E. Milligan, "Henry Solomon Wellcome," *Dictionary of Business Biography*, ed. D. J. Jeremy & C. Shaw, 5 (1986): 727–736; A. W. Haggis, "The Life and Work of Sir Henry Wellcome," unpublished typescript (WI, 1942).

6. D. S. L. Cardwell, *The Organisation of Science in England* (London, 1972), 175–176.

7. "Cosmo-pharmacy," *Chemist and Druggist* (20 May 1893): advertisement pp. 4–5. WF 84/7: 10 Chemical notebooks: Chemical Research Book 1 October 1889–31 October 1893, includes routine analyses e.g. of dyes from the firm and competitors.

8. E. M. Tansey "The Wellcome Physiological Research Laboratories 1894–1904: The Home Office, Pharmaceutical Firms, and Animal Experiments," *Medical History* 33 (1989): 1–41.

9. Milligan, "Wellcome" (n.5), 729–730.

10. "The anti-toxin treatment of diphtheria: The Supply of Serum," *British Medical Journal* 2 (1894): 1452.

11. "Report of the Lancet Special Commission on the relative strengths of diphtheria anti-toxic serums," *Lancet* 2 (1896): 182–195.

12. The Wellcome Physiological Research Laboratories (n.d.) WF: Strong Room 6, Drawer 1990: Papers *re* registration of WPRL, 1900–1901, henceforward WF: WPRL Registration. *Chemist and Druggist* (17 June 1899): 947.

13. *Chemist and Druggist* (11 November 1899): 780–781; W. Dowson *The Wellcome Physiological Research Laboratories* (London, c. 1902).
14. "Notes *re.* petition to Home Office" probably by Henry Wellcome 20 July 1900, WF: WPRL Registration (n.12).
15. Ibid. Parke, Davis and Company from America were praised in the British press for using such techniques, but no recognition was made of the difficulties that faced British manufacturers, e.g. "A chemist's trip to America," *Chemist and Druggist* (29 January 1898): 182–183; J. C. McWalter "Materia medica animalis," *Pharmaceutical Journal* (13 August 1898): 155–159.
16. Tansey "Laboratories" (n.8), 19–35.
17. "The standardising of drugs by experiments on animals," *British Medical Journal* 2 (1900): 447–448.
18. Home Office to Wellcome 5 September 1901 WF: WPRL Registration (n.12).
19. Wellcome to B. W. & Co. 27 January 1902 WF: B3 Letter/Memoranda Book 1901–1906, p.65.
20. J. Parascandola, "Industrial research comes of age: The American pharmaceutical industry 1920–1940," *Pharmacy in History* 27 (1985): 19–20; "The 'Preposterous Provision': The American Society for Pharmacology and Experimental Therapeutics' ban on industrial pharmacologists, 1908–1941," in this volume.
21. "The conference in London," *Chemist and Druggist* (23 June 1900): 1035.
22. Dale to Wellcome, 14 March 1906, WF: E2: 'The Wellcome Physiological Research Laboratories' 1895–1922.
23. Nobel Prize Winner in 1936. W. S. Feldberg "Henry Hallett Dale 1875–1968," *Biographical Memoirs of Fellows of the Royal Society* 16 (1970): 77–174. H. H. Dale, "Autobiographical sketch," *Perspectives in Biology and Medicine* 1 (1958): 129.
24. Dowson to Wellcome 11 February 1904 WI: WIHM: 86/18: WPRL material.
25. Dowson to Wellcome 27 February 1905 WF: K Letters from Dowson to Wellcome *re.* Liége exhibition and WPRL 1905. Barger was the chemist employed at the WPRL, see H. H. Dale "George Barger 1878–1939," *Obituary Notices of Fellows of the Royal Society* 3 (1941): 63–85.
26. Dowson to Wellcome (n.24) [same letter]. Dr. F. B. Power was the Director of WCRL.
27. These were A. J. Ewins, A. T. Glenny, J. Mellanby, G. Barger, E. Mellanby, H. H. Dale, P. P. Laidlaw, H. King, and J. H. Burn.
28. H. H. Dale "On Some Physiological Actions of Ergot," *Journal of Physiology* 34 (1906): 163–206 [esp. p.169].
29. H. H. Dale *The Wellcome Physiological Research Laboratories* (London, 1910), 9–10; see also J. R. Vane "The Research Heritage of Henry Wellcome," *Pharmaceutical Historian* 10 (1980): 2–8.
30. WF: C4: HSW/Friends/F. B. Power.
31. Ibid., WF: P6 Staff Biographies.
32. The celebrations were reported at length in *The Pharmaceutical Journal* (25 July 1896): 78–79.
33. Writing paper headed "The Wellcome Research Laboratories" was used by Power as late as 1901 (WF: D3 WCRL: Typescript History compiled c. 1927/1928).

34. *The Pharmaceutical Journal* (n.32)
35. Power to BW & Co, 22 January 1907 in WF: D3 WCRL (n.33). F. B. Power, *The Wellcome Chemical Research Laboratories* (London, 1900).
36. This collection, considerably enlarged, is still at the Wellcome Research Laboratories now at Beckenham.
37. WF: D3 WCRL (n.44); WF: P2 Staff record book. Printed lists and reprints in WF archives.
38. [Burroughs, Wellcome & Co.] *The Wellcome Chemical Research Laboratories. With a Description of the Exhibits of these Laboratories at the Anglo American Exposition, London, 1914* (London 1914), 7.
39. "Dr. F. B. Power. Obituary" *Nature* 119 (1927): 573. WF: K Typescript BW Historical Notes, 1930
40. *The Wellcome Chemical Laboratories* (n.38), 7–8.
41. The main source is WF: D3: WCRL: Private & Confidential Report on Formulae and Secret Processes, dated 13 January 1916. WF: B3: 'Chronology 1880–1936'.
42. *'Wellcome' Brand Chemical Price List* (1912), *passim*.
43. *Price List of Fine Products* (1913), 113–114, 157–158.
44. The work of the laboratories was displayed in all the great international exhibitions, and their prizes listed in company publications and advertisements.
45. Wellcome to Balfour, 8 February 1913, quoted by Haggis "Wellcome" (n.5), 413.
46. WF: B3: Chronology 1880–1936; C. Harington "The work of the National Institute for Medical Research" *Proc. R. Soc. Lond. B* 136 (1950): 333–348.
47. WF:C4: HSW/Friends/F. B. Power: Letter from Wellcome to Dr. Carl Alsberg Chief of Bureau of Chemistry, Department of Agriculture, Washington, D.C., 12 July 1915. Power donated his books to the Department of Pharmacy, University of Wisconsin, the nucleus of what is now the F. B. Power Pharmaceutical Library.
48. Macdonald, *In Pursuit of Excellence* (n.4) p.84; [Burroughs, Wellcome & Co.] *Therapeutic sera, vaccines and tuberculins* (Beckenham. c. 1922).
49. [The Wellcome Foundation] *The Wellcome Research Institution and the Affiliated Research Laboratories and Museums Founded by Henry S. Wellcome* (London, 1932) *passim*; C. H. Kellaway "The Wellcome Research Institution," *Proc. R. Soc. London B* 135 (1948): 259–270.
50. A. R. Hall & B. A. Bembridge, *Physic & Philanthropy: A history of the Wellcome Trust, 1936–1986* (Cambridge, 1986).
51. Ibid., pp.33–5.

The French Pharmaceutical Industry, 1919–1939

by Michael Robson

THE French pharmaceutical industry changed significantly during the 1920s and 1930s. The details of the adjustments made in the industry in response to various factors during this period sheds light on the unique nature of the French pharmaceutical industry. From a recent British perspective, France has not been seen as a significant producer of pharmaceuticals. Yet, in the late 1940s and early 1950s France boasted two local firms capable of manufacturing antibiotics—a reasonable record compared with the situation in Britain.[1] To clarify these differing views, this essay starts by examining the state of the French industry in 1919. It looks at legislation that shaped and restricted the industry up to that time, and assesses the impact of the First World War, concentrating on policy debates over the future of the industry.

The second section of this essay describes the state of the industry at the end of the inter-war period. To understand the inner workings of the pharmaceutical industry, it is important first to place the industry in the context of the French economy as a whole, as well as in the more general context of the European chemical industry.

The third section looks at the potential for growth in the industry during this period, by examining the particular constraints placed on French firms. Key factors here were government regulations and company structure. Commercial strategies, attitudes toward spending on research and development, and the impact of foreign competitors on the domestic market also played critical roles in the development of the pharmaceutical industry in France in the period between World War I and World War II (1919–1939).

State of the Pharmaceutical Industry in 1919

Two pieces of legislation defined the boundaries within which the French pharmaceutical industry operated at the beginning of the

68 Oldfield Grove, London SE16 2NB, England, and the London School of Economics.

inter-war period. The first of these was the "loi de Germinal" covering the practice of pharmacy. Enacted in 1803 in the Germinal month of the first French Republic, this law effectively resulted in a monopoly for the pharmacy profession by the late nineteenth century. By 1919 the law required all drug manufacturing on a factory scale to have the direct supervision of a pharmacist. This was in direct response to the appearance of pre-packaged medicines. The need for a supervising pharmacist tended to restrict the scale of manufacturing operations, placing a premium on the skills (or more importantly, the diploma) of the pharmacist, and generally precluded the continuing development of the industry along the lines followed by the Germans.[2]

The other long-standing piece of legislation affecting the pharmaceutical industry was the law on patents. The 1844 Patent Act specifically excluded medicines, on the grounds that it was immoral to allow monopolies to develop in this field.[3] Thus, the manufacturers' only protection for a new product was that offered by brand names. Although these were vigorously upheld, innovative companies regularly saw their efforts duplicated by competitors, who were able to market rival products with similar-sounding names.

The pharmaceutical companies working within these legal boundaries in 1919 fall into two principal categories. The primary producers of fine chemicals operated simple, fairly large-scale chemical processes to extract vegetable drugs such as quinine. They also refined and treated a range of inorganic products to make crystalline salts such as the bismuth compounds.[4] These companies were small and most were family run. That they were counterparts of the English and Scottish fine chemical companies can be seen through their common membership in international cartels and syndicates.[5]

The second group within the industry included the sera and vaccine producers. Growing out of the work of Pasteur, and later Brown-Séquard, these companies can be traced following the introduction of a registration system in 1895. Of the fifty-nine companies applying for permission to supply biological products between 1895 and 1920, twenty-nine were based in the Paris region, the other major center being Lyon.[6]

The two types of companies actually represent ends of a spectrum. Companies frequently manufactured a combination of fine chemicals and biological products. Those who were principally involved with the latter were usually distinguishable by the tendency to refer to themselves as "laboratories."

Two individual manufacturers stand out. The main supplier of medicinal fine chemicals was the Etablissements Poulenc Frères. They produced a wide range of chemicals and had been one of the first French companies to invest in research. Poulenc set up a company research center at Ivry near Paris in 1903.[7] Ernest Fourneau, a promising young pharmacist-chemist was appointed director, a post he held until leaving to join the Institut Pasteur in 1911. While at Ivry, Fourneau's main work involved the development of Poulenc's branded cocaine substitute, the local anaesthetic Stovaine. After he had moved to the Institut Pasteur, Fourneau maintained his personal contacts and the company continued to support some of his projects into the inter-war period.[9]

The other large manufacturer in this period was the Societé Chimique des Usines due Rhône (SCUR). SCUR had its earliest roots in France's first aniline dye companies, and in some ways resembled the diversified German companies.[10] However, SCUR differed in its weaker commitment to research. Based in Lyon and maintaining an interest in dyes and other fine chemicals, SCUR was isolated from the French tradition of manufacturing pharmacy by its chosen product range and location. During the first decades of the twentieth century, SCUR supplied pharmaceutical raw materials for proprietary manufacturers, without marketing their own medicines. The company was a member of some of the main pharmaceutical commodity cartels, and they were one of the few French manufacturers to produce synthetic antipyretics in the pre-war period.[11] Over the years SCUR built a reputation for pure products. It also gained a name for prudent financing, relying heavily on the re-investment of profits to fund growth.[12]

World War One. During the First World War the French pharmaceutical industry experienced major upheavals. In many cases companies had relied more heavily on German suppliers than they had been prepared to admit. In trying to boost production in the early months of the war one of the major problems was the shortage of labor.[13] An added problem was the growing shortage of raw materials and intermediates, prompting the government to set up the Office Nationale des Produits Chimiques et Pharmaceutiques in October 1914. This body, based in the Faculté de Pharmacie in Paris, was to carry out a survey of production capacity and to allocate raw material supplies where most needed.[14] The production census showed serious disruption and shortages developing. As might be expected, the allocation of scarce chemicals by the Office became a highly contentious issue, and manufacturers complained bitterly that only a small number were benefitting. In one publicly debated instance it was felt that the Office Nationale had unfairly handed SCUR a virtual monopoly of the French market for aspirin.[15]

Drugs of German origin continued to find their way into French pharmacies until well into the war. One importer, G. Doumas, was closely examined by the French Ministry of War after taking delivery of a total of eighteen tons of antipyretics. He was eventually judged to have acted in good faith, having believed them to be of Swiss manufacture. As for legitimate trade, British companies went some way towards meeting French requirements formerly supplied by the

Germans. The French particularly took supplies of British-made urotropine, sodium benzoate, and lanoline. However, tension developed between the Allies after the British government stopped exports of chemicals to France in 1918. In the case of quinine the French had seen the British making monopolistic profits, which they estimated at 40%, while France's main domestic producer, the Société de Traitement des Quinquinas, was starved of the necessary raw materials.[16]

The disruption of trade and shortages experienced during the war provoked discussion of the state of the French pharmaceutical industry. By airing general views, manufacturers sought to influence policy decisions in the post-war period. A survey carried out by the Société de Thérapeutique resulted in several specific proposals.[17] These included calls for the introduction of the patenting of the chemical processes for the production of pharmaceuticals, following the example of the Germans; the limiting of brand names to a period of fifteen years, after which presumably they would fall into the public domain; and the creation of a national laboratory for pharmacology, although partisans of the latter were divided as to whether it should be a research institute or a standards bureau.

One surprising result of the survey was the reaction of the small to medium-sized manufacturer. Although in favor of some deregulation, Adrian & Cie for instance, was reluctant to see changes in the patent law. The extension of patenting to include medicines would restrict their scope for launching new products according to their observation of the demand for rivals' preparations. It would also have required them to go through the formalities of registering their existing products. In their eyes, such a development could only lead to more work for the lawyers and they were already happy with the niche they had found for themselves in the industry. The larger manufacturers such as Poulenc and the Usines du Rhône tended to feel that patenting was necessary, that it would be a great help for them not to have to devise ways around the legislation on pharmacy, but that the creation of a national laboratory was largely irrelevant.[18]

The French Pharmaceutical Industry to 1938/39

Having summarized the legal restraints on pharmaceutical manufacturers, and described some of the rhetoric that set the tone for the post-war period, it is important to look more closely at the industry to get some measure of its size and significance.

By the inter-war period a sophisticated system had evolved to meet the demand for pharmaceutical products in France. Drugs were divided into "magistrale" preparations (pharmacopoeial drugs) and "specialités" (proprietary remedies). Traditionally, the manufacturers of the latter class divided themselves rather snobbishly according to further hierarchy. Specialities could be "scientifique" or "grand publique," distinguishing between ethical and non-ethical proprietaries. However, by the mid-1920s these distinctions were becoming blurred. Manufacturers of ethical proprietaries became more vertically integrated and involved with sales and marketing; those specializing in non-ethical products often diversified through buying in research or brand names of "scientific" specialities.

The tradition of branded specialities in France lies behind the commonly held belief that the French pharmaceutical industry grew out of pharmacy, whereas the German (and to a lesser extent the Swiss and the British) industry developed as an offshoot of the chemical industry.[19] The dominating position of the pharmacist in the French pharmaceutical industry is a recurring theme throughout the inter-war period.

By the late 1930s the annual consumption of "specialités" in France had reached FF 1.6 billion.[20] For the most part this demand was satisfied by French companies. However, in certain categories, notably the "scientific" proprietaries, the French were heavily dependent on foreign firms. The French subsidiaries of Swiss and German companies imported drugs in bulk, or in a semi-finished state for local packing or working up. By the mid 1930s the typical turnover of these foreign scientific firms was of the order of FF 8–25 million.[21] Roughly ten companies were involved. Some of the larger ones do not give figures, but it is likely that the sales of foreign drug companies in France grew to around FF 200 million by the late 1930s, of which 80% were ethical products. At this time the foreign drug companies dominated this market, and few of the local firms were involved in the scientific category at all. (Poulenc, Comar, and Roussel were the most notable exceptions.) The annual sales of locally made "scientific" products amounted to a total of around FF 150 million.

The rest of the French industry aimed to satisfy the public's demand for proprietary preparations. Products such as laxatives, cough medicines, tonics, and balms in various forms, some particularly French, sold well during the 1920s and 1930s. Encouraged by the advertising possibilities of the new communications media, a field that had been dominated by local pharmacists putting up their own concoctions to meet local tastes, became dominated by nationally marketed preparations.[22]

On the industry's export position, the French had a tradition of strong sales in South America, the rest of Europe, and the Far East. The Paris address on the packet was felt to be an advantage in the marketing of drugs during the 1920s and 1930s.[23] By 1938, an estimated 400 out of a total of 495 manufacturers surveyed, exported significant quantities of specialities.[24] This was a major increase from the fifty manufacturers who claimed to export in 1914.

The pattern of trade was very uneven during the inter-war period, partly as a result of the volatility of the franc on the international currency markets, and partly as a result of the world recession after 1929 and the resultant increase in protectionism.[25] While there were genuine attempts to establish international standards of drug purity and strength, many countries used the issue of purity as a further form of protection for their domestic industry. Importers were required to submit their products for lengthy and costly analyses before they were admitted. Often "unnecessary" imports of relatively luxurious items suffered first when countries re-assessed their trade positions, and French drug exports as a whole were badly affected.

By the mid 1930s manufacturers found themselves forced back into the French market. As the capital required to work a novel recipe for a speciality was quite small, and the profit margins were great, many had been attracted to the business in the meantime. Competition became acute. Even the manufacturers of "scientific" products were affected, as many had sought to smooth the financing of their research and development departments by selling one or two popular products as "cash cows."[26] By the late 1930s manufacturers themselves felt that they had done well—in some cases profits appear to have been breathtaking—but that the golden age of popular specialities was now drawing to a close.[27]

Industrial Context. A German survey published in 1930 estimated the global production of the chemical industry at a total of RM 22.05 billion or approximately £1.1 billion. The largest share of this output (34%) came from the heavy chemical sector. However, the second largest sub-total was the production of pharmaceutical products, consisting of the whole range from minerals to vegetable drugs, and from synthetic products to biological extracts. These amounted to 14% of world output in 1929.[28] Another survey divided the French chemical industry into sectors (Table 1) to try and assess the importance of chemicals to the French economy (a task the report described as "chimeric"). Meanwhile the same source placed France's chemical production lowest among the major producing countries in the late 1920s. The United States ranked first, with 45.8 percent of the total world chemical production in 1928; Germany, Great Britain, and France followed, with percentages of 16.7, 12.5, and 7.0, respectively.

It is quite possible that this survey for the Conseil Nationale Economique sought to exaggerate the importance of the chemical industry to the French economy. The author had been the head of the Office Nationale de Produits Chimiques et Pharmaceutiques, one of a number of bodies left over after the war with an interest in guaranteeing France's raw material supplies, as part of national security.[31] However, the figures give some idea of the place of the pharmaceutical sector within the general pattern. Although the em-

Table I. FRENCH CHEMICAL INDUSTRY (1930)[29]

Sub-sector	Number of firms (F)	Employees (E)	E/F
Heavy chem.	123	75 000	610
Drugs & Pharm.	256	22 000	86
Colors, Inks, Varnishes	267	14 000	52
Petrol	14	12 500	893
Dyestuffs	9	5 000	556
Explosives	15	3 700	247
Photographic products	13	3 500	269
Tanning	19	3 400	179
Synthetics	9	2 500	278
Soaps, Detergents	10	2 300	230
Wood distillation	13	1 400	108
Celluloid	11	700	64
Others	351	54 000	154
Total	1 100	200 000	182

ployee to firm (E/F) ratio can be misleading, it would seem that pharmaceutical companies were small, but that they were among the most numerous of companies in the chemical industry.

Geographically the pharmaceutical industry was based in the Paris region. Paris was the major market for drugs, with one doctor for every 300 inhabitants, and had good access to raw materials. Also, having a base in Paris allowed proximity to the Faculté de Pharmacie, which became increasingly important as the Faculté became a center for official regulation of the industry following the setting up of the Laboratoire Nationale there in 1926 As a result, 66% of the companies and 75% of the total workforce of the industry were centered on the Paris region.[32]

The Inter-War Period

Government/industry relations.   The actions of the French government affected the pharmaceutical industry during the inter-war period in two areas. The first of these consisted of laws (or proposed legal changes) in the 1920s that tinkered with the pharmacists' monopoly law. The second area where the French government overlapped with the pharmaceutical industry was in social and welfare legislation. This category includes Social Security laws, laws on taxation, and the introduction of price controls under the Front Populaire. These pieces of legislation date from the second half of the inter-war period.

In 1916, a pharmaceutical speciality was legally defined as "a product with curative or preventive properties having a particular brand name and for which the manufacturer claimed either priority of invention, sole ownership or superiority of action in advertising material."[33] However, manufacturers could not protect their specialities by keeping the contents secret, as the loi de Germinal specifically prohibited the sale of secret remedies. The law was modified in July 1926. Under the new law, specialities could avoid being classed as secret remedies if they carried the name of the manufacturer on the packing and a list of the contents was deposited at a government laboratory.

At the same time the Laboratoire National de Controle du Médicament was set up to handle registrations. This followed pressure from exporting companies who were coming up against trade barriers under which they had to prove that their products were officially recognized at home.[34]

One common complaint about the registration of specialities with the LNCM was the cost; each concentration and package had to be separately submitted at a cost of FF 20 a time. As one correspondent pointed out, "If we have to pay FF 6,000 for the right to sell compounded ampoules containing a variety of different ingredients, in a market such as Spain, we would prefer to give up the business and leave the field open to Fischer of Frankfurt or Parke-Davis of Detroit." Some countries, such as Greece, enforced stringent entry conditions as a disguised form of protectionism, and were unwilling even to accept certification from the LNCM. Here the ordinary manufacturer was at a disadvantage compared to the Institut Pasteur, whose sera and vaccines were universally welcome with purchasers feeling them to be guaranteed by the French State itself.

Registration and hence recognition was a crucial point in the evolution of pharmaceutical specialties. In the early 1920s they had enjoyed a shady semi-official existence. At that time numbers of preparations grew rapidly, and new breeds of wholesale companies and co-operatives had already begun to emerge. Interestingly the changes in the law were largely an acknowledgement of what had already happened.

One other aspect of the loi de Germinal under attack in the late 1920s was the ban on commercial partnerships between pharmacists and businessmen untrained in pharmacy. This had originally been conceived to prevent commercial considerations undermining professional decisions, and to act as a further guarantee of standards. Combined with the requirement for pharmaceutical production to be carried out under the direct supervision of a pharmacist, this seriously limited the scope for growth in the industry. Companies were forced to go to great lengths when forming partnerships to ensure that the board of directors of a company were all trained pharmacists. Following the merger of SCUR and Etablissements Poulenc Frères in 1928, a separate subsidiary, *Specia*, had to be set up to handle the pharmaceutical business.[35] Others disguised the fact that they had formed limited companies by avoiding calling themselves pharmaceutical manufacturers. Roussel was one such case where the pharmaceutical products were technically handled by the *Laboratoires* Français de Chimiothérapie, but mostly made by the *Usines Chimiques* des Laboratoires Français (UCLAF).[36]

One associated problem was that the "Société a Responsabilité Limité" (a form of limited liability company), which had been introduced to help smaller businesses raise capital, was not open to pharmaceutical manufacturers. Legal experts debated whether the law should be amended, and various bills were introduced. However, eventually it was concluded that limiting financial liability would compromise the principle of total responsibility for purity and safety that applied to vendors of medicines.

The French government introduced a national system of health insurance in 1928. Under the scheme insured persons purchased medicines at 15% of their face value.[37] The Faculté de Pharmacie was appointed to draw up a list of medicines covered by the scheme. The manufacturers first reacted to the news of a limited list with universal hostility. They felt it would undermine doctors' freedom to prescribe, and their own freedom on drug pricing.[38] However, the Faculté soon concluded that it was impossible to list "essential" preparations, and in practice the authorized list consisted of those products registered with the Laboratoire National. A rush to register products followed, although many of the smaller companies complained bitterly of the costs they incurred.[39]

The subject of the taxation of medicines was one that the French government had avoided repeatedly. The question had been considered in 1907 but was withdrawn after strong lobbying by the Chambre Syndicale des Fabricants de Produits Pharmaceutiques (the pharmaceutical manufacturers' union).[40] Generally it was felt to be a moral question: such a tax would hurt most those already disadvantaged through illness and probably unemployment. Products advertised to the general public were affected by a tax introduced in 1916. The main issue was raised again in the early 1930s. The projected "taxe unique" on medicines encountered much resistance, although faced with fiscal necessity moral arguments took second place. The plan involved taxing medicines at the place of production, leaving the original manufacturer to pass off some of the total onto the wholesaler and retailer. The government upset many vested interests by disturbing the delicately balanced system of discounts allowed between the various intermediaries and policed by the trade associations. After hard lobbying, the tax was eventually imposed but at a reduced rate in August, 1934.[41]

Finally the late 1930s saw a further spate of government interest in the pharmaceutical industry. Price control legislation was a mainstay of the Front Populaire government between 1936 and 1938. Medicines were one of the areas covered. Any price rises by manufacturers had to be justified before the Commission de Surveillance des Prix. Manufacturers were deterred from applying, given that a hearing with the Commission implied the full disclosure of cost details. The government was not alone in its hostility to the industry. A political consensus was established around the notion that drugs had been too expensive for too long. The manufacturers' response was to keep a low profile. Makers of ethical products felt that they could avoid the worst of any public backlash, but the manufacturers of popular proprietaries saw this as the end of a "Belle Epoque."[42]

In this atmosphere the government also managed to introduce a new, more sophisticated system of health insurance. The latter is particularly interesting in that the various schedules managed to classify drugs according to efficacy, where the earlier act had failed, and a sliding scale of reimbursement was introduced—a further confirmation that something had changed in the balance of power between the industry, the medical profession, and the government.[43]

In summary, the French industry was fairly successful at influencing changes in the law, or simply devising ways around it in the first half of the inter-war period. However, the industry was much less effective in turning later changes to its advantage.

Strategy and Structure. As described earlier, the inter-war period saw rapid growth in the numbers of pharmaceutical specialities on the market. This had strategic implications for the companies involved in the industry.

The main directory of specialities, the *Dictionnaire Vidal*, first appeared in 1911. By 1920 it featured approximately 1,400 entries. This had risen to 1,900 by 1925, 2,700 by 1929, and 5,600 by 1935.[44] This represented only a fraction of the total. A report of the Conseil Economique et Sociale published in 1948, based on figures from the Laboratoire Nationale, estimated that immediately before the Second World War there were around 30,000 specialities registered for sale in France.[45] Various company records put the figure even higher at around 45,000.[46] Although the number of products grew rapidly, relatively few of the specialities counted were related to major therapeutic advances of the period: vitamins, insulin, synthetic antimalarials, and later the sulphonamides. For the most part, specialities involved slight modifications in the formulation of known remedies, mixtures of likely ingredients. Also common was the launching of competing brands with the name of the laboratory attached to a widely used generic name. In this way Vidal includes nine different brands of adrenaline under names such as "adrenaline Clin." Variations in the entries for particular companies are not necessarily meaningful; entries in the directory were paid for by the companies and if they felt Vidal was overcharging, manufacturers were inclined to pull out. To get an idea of the scale of charges, the Swiss firm Sandoz paid over FF 2,000 annually for their fourteen entries in the mid 1930s, equivalent to the cost of one travelling salesman.[48]

A significant amount of the growth experienced by the pharmaceutical companies during the period resulted from mergers. This was due in part at least to the legal restrictions on partnerships. Legally, each manufacturing unit required one pharmacist and one pharmacist could not reasonably control a production plant above a certain size. As companies could not grow "organically" they tended to take the alternative path of growth by acquisition.

The largest merger in the sector during the inter-war period was that which formed Rhône-Poulenc.[49] Such a maneuver required government sanction to waive the law on taxation of liquidated companies. The French government felt this merger was in the public interest, despite the administration's expressed ambivalence towards concentration within industries. As a rationalization, the merger made commercial sense since the companies had complementary ranges of products. It was also felt that it would help the two large French companies to compete on the international scene beginning to be dominated by IG Farben, the Swiss companies, and ICI.[50]

On a much smaller scale, Roussel was busily buying up laboratories, and hence brand names, with the cash generated by his successful anti-anemic speciality, Hémostyl.[51] The older companies tended to acquire brands in a more sedate manner. The product range of the Comar company in the early 1930s featured four principal brands that had been assembled, either bought outright or owned by silent partners, over a period of 30 or 40 years.[52] The intricacy of this small scale merger activity makes the French pharmaceutical industry particularly difficult to study from the outside. The various laboratories were owned in complicated patterns often by apparently unrelated companies.

Growth in the number of products and restructuring through mergers from the early 1920s leads to a second theme within commercial strategy: price regulation. As a proprietary became well known on a national scale, alternative brands became increasingly available. Cases of illegal substitution and price cutting began to occur and some form of regulation became desirable.

The first attempt to control substitution and price cutting had been made in 1899, with the "primes Lorette" system.[53] A second initiative came in 1907 with the "ticketistes," but it was not until the later Syndicat Générale de la Reglementation (S.G.R.) that the manufacturers managed to ensure that drugs available in pharmacies were unadulterated, made by the manufacturer stated, and sold at a standard price.[54] From their side, the retailers formed the Syndicat National de la Reglementation (N.R.) in 1910.[55] Together these bodies had the power to bring pressure to bear on recalcitrant pharmacists, with the ultimate sanction being the coordinated withholding of supplies of specialities to those persistently undercutting. By 1922 the S.G.R. claimed to have 261 members and the figures given for the sales of their special stamps indicate that by the mid-1920s specialities worth FF 150 million were sold under the S.G.R. scheme.[56] These regulatory bodies provided an additional service in chasing up cases of the illegal export of drugs from areas such as France where they were relatively cheap to areas where they were expensive such as eastern Europe.[57]

Informal groups of manufacturers tended to form within the framework of the regulatory bodies. The names of those involved with the older companies reappear throughout the proceedings and reports of the various institutions of the industry. Although networks are difficult to trace within these institutions, by the late 1930s one group of friends was meeting in an attempt to set up an independent co-operative wholesaler to challenge the Office Commerciale Pharmaceutique, then the largest distributor.[58]

The inter-war period then saw several changes in corporate structure and commercial strategy. The two were often closely linked. With exponential growth in the number of specialities on the market, companies pursued a vigorous policy toward establishing their own new brands. Several large mergers occurred, together with many smaller ones, due in part to external constraints on growth. A very small number of relatively large manufacturers were operating in the pharmaceutical industry during the period, together with a large number of small laboratories. This pattern was seen in other French industries. Small family-run businesses and larger rather diffuse holding companies co-existed for instance in the steel and engineering sectors.[59] However, more important than size was the division between the manufacturers of "scientific" and "popular" products. Despite the fact that the latter were often larger, they made little contribution to research and usually failed to capitalize on the success of their main products, tending to disappear with their products after a lifespan of twenty years. Finally, collusion between firms is evident in the first appearance of price-fixing and other regulatory bodies during the period. Other collusive practices such as cartellization are not so obvious, although Rhône-Poulenc is known to have signed international agreements in several cases. On the whole, attempts to reduce the level of competition within the French domestic market do not appear to have been successful, particularly if the accounts of the participants during the late 1930s are to be believed.

Conclusion

During the inter-war period French pharmaceutical companies were fairly small. They operated in a competitive domestic market, while also exporting a significant proportion of their output. As a result of legal restrictions on the types of business structure that could be used by the industry, the companies became rather secretive about the forms adopted and the manufacturing actually undertaken by subsidiaries. This makes historical unravelling difficult but not impossible. Throughout the period the influence of the Faculté de Pharmacie in Paris appears to have been strong, both as a result of the loi de Germinal, and later the setting up of the LNCM based in the Faculté.

In many ways the French companies were rather insular in their outlook. Few saw themselves as being involved in the same business as the large dyestuffs-to-pharmaceuticals companies that had evolved in Germany and elsewhere.[60] Fewer still spent money on research. As Sandoz observed at the end of the 1930s, many French companies were beginning to suffer from a public backlash at the high level of profits that had been made, without the manufacturers being able to point to the need to re-invest as an excuse for high prices.

From an examination of company sources it emerges that the French pharmaceutical industry was still a minor force on the international scene in the late 1930s. Its study, however, is rewarding as an example of the interaction between government and industry in a potentially advanced technological sector and of that between small companies struggling for business in a competitive environment.

Notes and References

1. J. M. Liebenau, "The British Success with Penicillin," *Social Studies of Science* 17 (1987): 69–86.
2. J. Sigvard, "L'industrie du médicament en France; quelques points d'histoire," *Bull. Acad. Nat. Med.* 166 (1982): 829–834.
3. See also G. Dillemann, "Les remèdes secrets et la reglementation de la pharmacopée Française," *Revue d'Histoire de la Pharmacie* 23 (Mars 1976).
4. A. Haller, *Exposition Universelle Internationale de 1900: Les Industries Chimiques* (Paris, 1903).
5. Darrasse and Roques were two French companies in the camphor producers' group, the British members of which included Whiffen, May & Baker, and Howard. Greater London Record Office, B/WHF Collection.
6. Archives Nationales, Paris (AN), SAN 5127.
7. Lomueller, "Histoire de la SA les Ets POULENC Freres" (n.d., manuscript at Rhone-Poulenc head office, Quai Paul Doumer, Courbevoie, Paris); see also AN (n. 6), 65 AQ P631.
8. H. J. Barber, *Essays in the History of Chemotherapy* (Dagenham: May & Baker, 1979); R. Fabre, *Figures Pharmaceutiques Françaises: Notes Historiques et Portraits,* (Paris: Masson, 1953).
9. J. P. Billon, "La decouverte des sulfamides: Implications et contributions de l'industrie," paper given at Institut Pasteur Colloque 6/11/85 to mark the fiftieth anniversary of the discovery of sulphonamides.
10. L. F. Haber, *The Chemical Industry 1900–1930* (Oxford: Clarendon Press, 1971), p. 159.

11. That SCUR was a member of the antipyretics cartel can be shown from some of the cartel documents in CIBA-Geigy group archives, Basel.

12. Crédit Lyonnais archives, avenue du Coq, Paris 75008, dossier 38722, including cuttings from *A.E.F.*, 8/8/23.

13. The French chemical industry as a whole experienced a reduction in its workforce of 30% in August 1914. AN, F 12 8018 2/7.

14. AN, F 12 7703. On the general influence of the Faculté de Pharmacie see G. Valette, ed. *La Faculté de Pharmacie de Paris, 1882–1982* (Paris: Comarco, 1982).

15. *La Chronique Pharmaceutique, 12*, Mai 1918.

16. AN, F 12 7710.

17. *Bulletin de la Société de Thérapeutique* 20 (1915): 218–255.

18. Ibid.

19. This comment was made very frequently in personal interviews with senior representatives of pharmaceutical companies (Rhone-Poulenc, Dausse, Comar, Roussel-UCLAF) carried out during 1985. The only published version of this is an incidental comment by K. Blunden in *Etude sur l'évolution de la concentration dans l'industrie pharmaceutique en France* (Office des Publications Officielles des Communautes Europeennes, 1975).

20. £ 1 = FF 86. Y. Baudouin, *Commission consultative de dommages et des réparations. Monogr. A. I. 39 Industrie Pharmaceutique* (Impr. Nat., 1948).

21. The French subsidiaries of CIBA and Sandoz have been studied particularly closely. These had turnovers of around FF 10 million. They clearly felt they were smaller than Roche and the main German group, IG Farben.

22. G. Thuillier, *Pour une histoire du cotidien au XIXème siècle en Nivernais* (Paris: Mouton, 1977).

23. The commercial allure of a Paris address was discussed by Sandoz' Paris subsidiary. See Sandoz company archives, Basel, Switzerland, H 104.19, "Dr. Court's Report, No 46. Paris April 1926."

24. Baudouin, *Commission consultative*, (n.20).

25. The impact of both these factors is chronicled throughout the inter-war period in the Bulletin Mensuel de la Chambre Syndicale des Fabricants de Produits Pharmaceutiques (*Bull. Mens.*).

26. Roche were quoted as one example by Sandoz' Paris subsidiary. See Sandoz archives, H 104.19, "Dr. Court's Report No 34, Espagne et Sous-organisations en generale, January 1926."

27. Profits were claimed to have been of the order of 5 to 600%. See Sandoz archives, H 104.19, internal memo "Prix et Démarches à la Commission de Controle, France 1938."

28. M. Roth in *Chemiker Zeitung*, cited in "La Situation des principales branches de l'Economie nationale," *Journal Officiel* (JO), 4/12/32.

29. JO, 4/12/32.

30. For comparison, at this period Levy-Leboyer put French employment in industry at around 4.5 million (although in the case of pharmaceuticals many employees may be classed by him as small artisans), see M. Levy-Leboyer, "Innovation and Business Strategies in 19th and 20th Century France," in Carter, Forster and Moody ed., *Enterprise and Entrepreneurs in 19th and 20th Century France* (Baltimore: Johns Hopkins, 1976).

31. Other bodies included the related Office des Matieres Premieres pour la Droguerie run by Professor Perrot which considered the economic consequences of new developments in materia medica. See Sandoz archives, H 104.19, "Entretien avec Prof. Perrot 20/11/29."

32. Baudouin, *Commission consultative*, (n.20). The central role of Paris is considered further in J. Laurent, *La Pharmacie en France* (Paris, thesis, 1959).

33. Sigvard, "L'industrie due médicament," (n.2).

34. JO, 25/7/1926; *Bull. Mens.*, 1926, p.143. Poplanski wrote that a "certain tolerance was shown to such companies which were illegal but whose disappearance would cause distress to the general public" cited in M. Audinot, *La Pharmacie et L'Industrie Pharmaceutique* (Doctoral Thesis, Paris, 1968).

35. M. Lachaux, "Le President Francois Albert Buisson" (paper given at L'Academie Nationale de Pharmacie, 9/1/85).

36. Information supplied by Dr. Jeannin, acting archivist, Roussel-Uclaf, Paris, October, 1985.

37. This superceded the provision made under the system of Assistance Medicale Gratuite instituted during the 1890s. See G. Thuillier, *Histoire*, (n.22).

38. Sigvard, "L'industrie du médicament," (n.2).

39. Sandoz were caught out by the rush to register products under the new system in January 1932.

40. Sigvard, "L'industrie du médicament," (n.2).

41. See *Bull. Mens.* throughout 1934.

42. Sandoz archives, H 104.19, "Prix et Demarches."

43. *AN*, files SAN 5144. Under the new system, Dausse for instance had the following profile:

Category	Numbers of Products
(Most essential) 1	0
2	92
3	55
(least essential) 4	33

44. L. Vidal and M. Dareau (eds.) *Dictionnaire de Specialites Pharmaceutiques* (Paris: Office de Vulgarisation Pharmaceutique, 1920). The collection of old copies of Vidal are held by the current publishers, 11 r Quentin Bauchart, 75008 Paris.

45. *Journal Officiel*, 12/3/1948. This report criticizes the pre-war industry particularly for the prevalence of "me-too" products.

46. Sandoz archives, H 104.19, Dr. Court's visit to Paris, January 1932.

47. LNCM archives are in the Archives Nationales, SAN category.

48. Sandoz archives, H 104.19, "Dr. Court's Report, France, December 1934."

49. Credit Lyonnais (Paris) dossier CL 38722, *AEF* cutting, nd, "c'est de la bonne rationalisation." On the relative strengths of the two, AEF felt that Poulenc were the weaker. See also Archives Nationales, 65 AQ P269.

50. M. Levey-Leboyer in A. D. Chandler and H. Daems (eds.), *Managerial Hierarchies* (1981).

51. Information supplied by Dr. Jeannin.

52. Comar company Board Minutes at Sanofi, 66, Avenue Marceau, Paris, 75008.
53. J. Sigvard, *Syndicat Nationale de L'Industrie Pharmaceutique* (Paris: SNIP, 1980).
54. The manufacturer's nightmare was the example of Italy where not even Bayer Aspirin, or Schering Atophan (both respected trade marks for pioneering drugs) could hold their own against local copies such as "Aspirolina" or "Nervonal;" *Bull. Mens.*, (1927), p.61–63.
55. Sigvard, *Syndicat Nationale*, (n.53).
56. Advertising material in *La Revue des Specialites*, (1925), January.
57. Concurrence Deloyale as it was known was a particular nuisance between France and Belgium, and France and Spain.
58. Sandoz archives, H 104.19, "Telephone de M. Gentil, 10/6/38."
59. D. Landes, "French Business," in E. M. Earle (ed.), *Problems of the 3rd and 4th Republics* (Princeton: Princeton University Press, 1951).
60. J. M. Liebenau (ed.), *The Challenge of New Technology*, (Aldershot: Gower, 1987).

Pro Medico, *1938.*

The Twentieth-Century British Pharmaceutical Industry in International Context

by Jonathan Liebenau

THE British pharmaceutical industry was roundly criticized after the Second World War for their failure to produce penicillin on a large enough scale to treat more than highest priority cases. In 1954, when Beechams paid a rather high price to their American competitor Pfizer for license to use the deep fermentation process, a cost was associated with this inadequacy and shame was brought to the industry. Since that time penicillin has been constantly used as a prime example of the inability of British industry to develop their own inventions, and of the pattern for British inventions to be exploited in the United States. In medicine alone this pattern has been followed numerous times, as for instance with the CAT scanner.[1]

This viewpoint needs to be analyzed. First, it is appropriate to ask to what extent this is a fair representation of events. Next, to the extent that it is accurate, it is necessary to account for its occurrence. This I propose to do by assessing the state of the industry leading up to the immediate postwar period, and analyzing the extent to which it was capable of effecting major development programs.

Here we will consider some key examples of new products that affected the conduct of British business, and illuminate the state of the industry and its international context throughout the middle of the twentieth century. Starting with Salvarsan, the antisyphilitic from Germany, we will then discuss insulin from Canada, the sulfonamides which in Britain were most influenced by French development, and finally penicillin. This work stems largely from recent research in British company archives.

Department of Information Systems, London School of Economics, Houghton Street, London WC2A 2AE, England.

Background

The British pharmaceutical industry in the nineteenth century was composed of a number of small firms serving domestic consumers and exporting to traditional markets, as Roy Porter describes elsewhere in this volume. They relied largely on raw materials imported from trading nations and tropical colonies or on standard chemicals and byproducts. The typical range of products included galenical preparations, alkaloids, numerous creams, dressings, and hundreds of miscellaneous medications. Leading firms such as Whiffen, Morson, Allen & Hanbury, May & Baker, and others all dealt in largely the same sort of products. By the 1830s some companies specialized in product areas such as the alkaloids for Morson's in London and Macfarlan's in Edinburgh, but for the most part the products overlapped among the competing firms. They also often listed a full range of medicines and acted as suppliers of products from associated companies where they could not cover the range adequately themselves.[2]

All of these companies were small, usually employing fewer than 100 workers, and with the exception of a small number of scientifically minded proprietors such as William Allen or Thomas Morson, there was little commitment to pharmaceutical investigation or product development. Even those who did establish laboratories did not integrate them into the normal course of business. This began to change with the grounding in 1894 of the Wellcome Physiological Research Laboratories, as Tilly Tansey and Rosemary Milligan explain in this volume. Although the Burroughs Wellcome laboratories were a response to the bacteriological and immunological work that had led to the development and commercialization of diphtheria antitoxin in Germany and France, Henry Wellcome did not model his laboratory after the established company research and development facilities at Hoechst or Bayer.

Instead, by the end of the nineteenth century the major British pharmaceutical firms were relying on cartel, convention, and licensing arrangements with German and Swiss companies to be able to offer new products. Upon the outbreak of the First World War the industry was, in business terms, reasonably stable but unable to supply the domestic market with many of the products that had so changed the industry abroad. There were no major industrial laboratories for product development, and British manufacturers, which had been complimented at numerous trade exhibitions for the quality of their standard products, seemed incapable of doing much else. This inability was recognized and much commented upon, but little changed. During the First World War they continued to get shipments from Continental suppliers while publicly resolving to rectify their inadequacies. Major contracts to supply the armed forces had to be given to United States companies, and even UK subsidiaries of U.S. manufacturers such as Parke Davis & Co. and Mulford did a booming business.[3]

Salvarsan

The response of the industry to Salvarsan (arsphenamine) was meant to be a turning point. Announced to the world by Paul Ehrlich in 1910 and tested amid enthusiastic publicity, Salvarsan was only just beginning to be relied upon on a large scale by the outbreak of war. Within a year the interrupted dependency on German supplies became a cause célèbre. By joining the list of key products which Britain relied on Germany for: dyestuffs, gyroscopes, optics, etc., Salvarsan became a symbol of British industry's inability to hold its own. The patents covering Salvarsan's production were available for abrogating but the technical ability was not in place. Only Burroughs Wellcome was capable of making Salvarsan in 1914 and they supplied their brand Kharsivan within a year.[4]

After hurriedly organizing a team in coordination with Poulenc Frères of Paris and concentrating for most of a year on the one project, May & Baker was able to produce Salvarsan by 1916. But problems persisted, and six years after the development of the most celebrated medicine of its day, quality control was poor. That they were able to do it at all is something of a tribute, but then a small American laboratory was successful before them, and French and Japanese Salvarsan were also available in 1915.

What was done with Salvarsan is also significant. The product had a peculiar status in many ways. With the special need for Salvarsan already identified, the newly formed Medical Research Committee [MRC] took an active role in regulating it. In collaboration with the Board of Trade, which coordinated the seizure of enemy-held properties including patents, licenses were granted to Burroughs Wellcome and Poulenc Frères to produce Salvarsan for the British market. The companies were held to the unique provision, however, that all samples "be submitted to biological tests" by the MRC. Official certificates were granted by the committee for each batch, but the cost of testing was charged to the manufacturers. The whole procedure was undertaken in a new government laboratory that maintained good contact with Burroughs Wellcome in particular. This arrangement seemed to function well for all parties involved, and within a year the MRC was petitioning the government to extend regulations to cover sera, vaccines, other biologicals, chemotherapeutics, and certain new medicines as they entered the market. Leading British medical scientists saw this as a move both to bring the UK into line with other countries whose products were regulated, and to put an end to a "period of anarchy."[5]

Aside from criticisms against patent medicine makers, the proliferation of new, science-based drugs merited suspicion. The pro-

fessor of pharmacology at University College, London, voiced some
of these concerns in a 1923 speech to the Royal Society of Medicine.
"Although the capitalization of the drugs industry has rendered important services to medicine it is idle to deny that it has also introduced serious new evils." And the law was unable to respond.
These evils, he believed, included the propensity of manufacturers
to:

select a new scientific discovery, which is a novelty and whose powers are
still undefined. It is a great advantage of course if the substance is such that
there is no easy method of testing its purity or activity. The rest is easy—
a commercial interest is there ready to boom the preparation and it is
nobody's business to check the statements made.[6]

The industry as such was almost wholly unregulated at the time,
with the exception of laws preventing the sale of contaminated items,
for which Britain had been a pioneer in the nineteenth century. The
sale of poisons was controlled and laws intending to curb opium
abuse were tried at various times. Drug adulteration was illegal, but
prosecutions were rare and almost never affected leading producers.
Nevertheless, it was not all that clear whether selling a medicine
that differed substantially from its *British Pharmacopoeia* description was illegal. In various test cases pharmacists were usually able
to argue either that the customer had not really specified that medicine exactly, or that the *Pharmacopoeia* did not have what was
needed.

Changes in the law had to wait a bit longer, but in 1921 two reports
had already laid the groundwork for British legislation.[7] Britain, they
claimed, was the only one "among the great nations" to have no
system of standards and no machinery for selecting or adopting any
standard. Britain's dependence upon the United States and Germany in this regard was seen as "discreditable to our national position in the world of science and a source of grave danger to the
community." The Therapeutic Substances Act, based on German
and American models, was finally passed in 1925 after being delayed
by three dissolutions of Parliament.

By the inter-war period, when the potential market for many new
remedies was opening up worldwide, national standards and regulations comparable with the United States and Germany were in
place in Britain. British legislation on new medicines trailed Germany by 30 years, and similar American legislation by twenty-three
years. Only with the War and subsequent fears of industrial dependence and shortage were there serious calls for regulations. By that
time it was necessary for leading British companies to be able to
assure domestic and foreign physicians that their products were
adequately tested and officially certified.

With the defeat of Germany and the destruction of their export
capacity, opportunities to build up the British pharmaceutical industry were boundless. Some commentators noted that British man-

ufacturers could not only retrieve that part of their domestic market lost to import penetration and established subsidiaries of German and Swiss manufacturers before the War, but expand significantly because of the vacuum created by Germany's inability to export in the postwar years. At the time, however, the situation looked quite different to those involved. There was still a serious problem about catching up to where the leading manufacturers had been before the outbreak of war, and a shortage of trained personnel compounded the feeling of disadvantage. Furthermore, many company heads thought that business had to be reestablished along previous lines before launching out in new directions. With trade unthreatened, the most attractive option for the proprietors of small companies was to get things back to their previous footing and then leave them there. That seemed difficult enough given postwar economic conditions.

Insulin

The case of the response to insulin is particularly illustrative of both official and commercial reactions to new products.[8] Developed at the University of Toronto in 1921/22, insulin immediately attracted attention in Canada and the United States. By the summer of 1922, officials at the Medical Research Council had taken an intense interest in insulin, partly as a response to its general promise but more particularly because there was an indication that Toronto wished to offer them British patent rights for insulin. The Toronto researchers, Banting, Best, and MacLeod, already had arranged with the Eli Lilly Company to manufacture and distribute in North America, and there was the possibility that the MRC might have a comparable role in Europe.

The MRC was hesitant. Accepting responsibility for a patent under the best of circumstances was liable to be tricky. There were two additional issues that made these arrangements especially difficult: the possibility that the patents might be inadequate, and the unprecedented difficulties associated with supervising and controlling commercially the production. There was one other consideration: the reluctance to accept foreign standards.

Two potential models were presented by recent past experiences, diphtheria antitoxin and Salvarsan. Both had been introduced with corporate support, were encouraged by public health authorities, needed standardization, and invited regulation. The first U.S. regulatory body for medicines, the Hygienic Laboratory of the United States Public Health Service, had been established to test and regulate the production of diphtheria antitoxin, and when Henry Dale, then of the MRC, visited Washington in 1922 to discuss insulin, the issue of antitoxin and Salvarsan arose. Although the Hygienic Laboratory was limited by statute over what it could regulate, their interest was identical to the British National Institute for Medical Research of the MRC, which would have been able to take on the task of regulating insulin. The similarity between the situation of insulin and that of antitoxin and Salvarsan extended to the character of the patent coverage, which in all three cases failed to include sufficient information about production methods. A subsidiary issue was the need for legislation to test products and license manufacturers. While the United States legislation was clear with regard to antitoxins and antisyphilitic products, it was not flexible enough to include insulin. Nevertheless, the form of American law and the role of the Hygienic Laboratory provided a model for new British regulatory authority which the MRC was encouraging. This was one further opportunity to "lend weight to contemplated legislation."

The holding of the Patent would simply regularize and define the Council's authority in relation to the insulin work. If the position were handled firmly and wisely, and with an obvious desire to help and not merely to restrict manufacture, it seems probable that the makers would submit to control as willingly as they still do in the case of the Salvarsan products, in connexion with which the legal authority for the Council's control has become more nebulous as the control has become more effective.[9]

Insulin could, it seemed, serve a number of related purposes by setting precedents and providing a new mechanism for supply as well as control.

These advantages, however, did not work to everyone's favor. Unsurprisingly, problems arose about how to regulate supply and who would be willing to produce under the MRC's restrictions. Less predictably, there was a general outcry about the possibility that the MRC would sanction patenting.

Initial approaches were made to British Drug Houses [BDH], Burroughs Wellcome, and Allen & Hanbury, and later arrangements were reached with Boots and Evans. In 1925, then, with the passage of the Therapeutic Substances Act, the MRC took responsibility for licensing these manufacturers, testing batches, and protecting the industry from imported insulin. Protection became a heated issue when it was claimed that the companies were in danger of being undersold by Danish suppliers, and debates raged for the next ten years as to whether the MRC was in its rights to take such control.

This issue came to a head in 1934 when Parliament considered lifting the tax on imported insulin, after complaints that lower prices were being discouraged by the lack of foreign competition. In a statement to Parliament by BDH, the wartime experiences were used to justify a special place for drugs makers. By pointing out that the postwar Safeguarding of Industries Act "was designed to safeguard and foster the products of the fine chemical industry in order to secure British independence," BDH was referring to the origins of post laissez-faire policy. Before the War, they argued, "the fine chemical and dyestuffs industries in this country had suffered so severely from German competition that they were in danger of extinction, . . . It is no less true today than it was then that for the retention of British initiative in research and in furthering the manufacture of fine chemicals the industry as a whole needs to be safeguarded."[10]

There was some strength to this argument for the case of insulin, although the argument has so frequently been used by the pharmaceutical industry that its impact has paled into cliché. Through MRC research, as much as improved production techniques, the price of British insulin had indeed fallen dramatically. "In order that there may be assured to the British diabetic a constant supply of reliable, high quality insulin prepared under accurate scientific control," BDH argued, "it is absolutely necessary that the industry should be protected from unregulated price competition." On the eve of the Second World War, British industry still seemed unable to look after itself.

M&B 693

In 1935 the anti-streptococcal drug Prontosil was developed in Germany, stimulating further work in France on sulfonamide compounds. Prontosil was adequately protected by patents, but the possibility of patenting variations stimulated further research in France. Coming not long after Rhône Poulenc took control of May & Baker, it seemed appropriate to use their reasonably well-equipped laboratories for further work in that area. Work began in 1936 and within two years a major new sulfonamide was developed, M&B 693. This compound proved effective against pneumococci, staphylococci, streptococci, meningococci, and gonococci. Heralded as a major breakthrough, this successful variation on German and French work brought immediate benefit to the company and changed the image of the industry's research and development capabilities.[12] Its importance is undeniable, but perhaps it did something of a disservice to the industry by providing a misleading sense of self-confidence.

M&B 693 is still regarded in the hagiography of British medical achievements as a great breakthrough, though the story is seldom told with full details about the role of the French corporate instigators. The importance of this is in part to show that British scientists relied to a large degree upon foreign developments, and also to show that it was only a breakthrough, not insignificantly a German one, that galvanized French and British reaction.

Research Capacity at the End of the Inter-War Period and Penicillin

A survey of the research capacity of five of the leading British pharmaceutical companies was carried out in 1942 for the newly

established consortium of British pharmaceutical manufacturers.[13]
This showed a wide variance in size and emphasis. In the period
1936 to 1941, May & Baker held the lead in the group for the number
of British patent applications (forty), but their publication rate was
slow, having produced only eleven scholarly articles out of a staff
of fifty-eight university graduates, fifteen of whom held doctorates.
Burroughs Wellcome had placed only six patent applications over
the period, but their sixty-six degree-holding scientific staff, twenty-
four of whom held doctorates, had published 220 journal articles
in the period. Glaxo stood between these two research leaders with
a less well qualified scientific staff (eight doctorates) but a publication record of thirty-four articles, and thirteen British patent applications. For the same period BDH had only five doctorates but
produced thirty-two publications, and seven patents. Even so they
were generally regarded as having little research potential. Boots
was similarly regarded. They had a very large staff of 269 scientific
workers, twenty-four of whom held doctorates. But they still published only 190 articles and applied for twelve patents over the five-
year period.

Research capacity is difficult to identify, and even more difficult
to quantify, so the figures above require a great deal of interpretation.
For one thing, the publication behavior of corporate scientists is to
a large extent dependent upon company policy. Nevertheless, the
ability to publish has long been regarded as an incentive for scientific
staff and this reflects on the esteem in which the company held them
as individual researchers. Patenting behavior is similarly dependent
upon corporate policy, and more specifically on the patenting patterns exhibited by competitors in closely allied areas. Nevertheless,
as with publications, these companies can be roughly compared as
to their interest in working at the forefront of research, as opposed
to allowing their product development efforts to trail behind acknowledged leaders. The number of people employed in scientific
staffs, and more particularly those with doctorates, is a better indicator of the effort individual companies placed in research. The
surprisingly large numbers of doctorate holders in Burroughs Wellcome and May & Baker is an indicator of the esteem with which
both companies held scientific research. Although Boots hired as
many potential research scientists as Wellcome, they formed a small
proportion of the total scientific staff of the company and they were
clearly not afforded the independence of other company scientists,
a stand perhaps appropriate for a company largely concerned then,
as today, with the retail end of the business.

It was in this context that efforts to capitalize on penicillin took
place. In 1941, as a response to the general feeling of inadequacy
in the industry, the Therapeutic Research Corporation [TRC] was
formed by the five companies above to coordinate certain aspects
of pharmaceutical research and development. Although the initial

intentions were broad, the TRC soon focused on the problem of bringing penicillin from an inconsistently produced research laboratory product to large scale manufacture. A number of problems became apparent immediately. One was the unprecedented difficulty of coordinating commercial activity, further aggravated by the obvious wartime hardships. Another was the feeling that a synthetic penicillin would be produced within a couple of years, which would obviate the need for massive development of cultured penicillin. A further problem was the perceived threat from the United States, where larger scale and better coordinated research and production would present an awesome commercial threat.

Despite these misgivings the five set out, with ICI's cooperation, to develop new production methods and meet the goal of supplying the armed forces with enough penicillin for the war wounded. Working through the most difficult conditions caused by the wartime economy, the TRC achieved a modicum of success. By 1944, however, twenty-five American companies (virtually every major pharmaceutical manufacturer) were connected in a network to exchange information and set standards for the mass production of penicillin. In the meantime, commercial problems in Britain associated with the TRC's effort were never completely solved. Some issues such as the disposition of patents were worked out amicably, but claims more narrowly associated with commercial and scientific prestige were more contentious. Suspicion about the intentions of ICI were particularly divisive, blunting any effort to present a unified optimistic picture to the British government and public. The official policy of endorsing the control of penicillin production by the TRC, but not adequately supporting the effort, became a subject of controversy as soon as American progress was known. The debate appeared in letters to The [London] Times and was argued in Parliament. One member of Parliament interpreted the situation as a case where a monopoly had been given to a small number of British firms that had little interest in surging ahead with new developments. In the United States, he claimed, there was a more competitive climate where twenty companies were racing to be the first mass producers.

I see the contrast in a different way. In Britain the five companies that formed the TRC were unable to avoid competing. In contrast, the American effort was tightly controlled by the government. The bitterness felt by the medical community was acute.

Conclusion

The British industry was not very healthy through the 1950s, though some important antibiotic and cortisone work was highly successful. Demoralized by the criticisms associated with penicillin and insecure of its place within the NHS, the nadir was reached around 1960, partly as the result of another foreign-developed product, Thalidomide. By rebuilding slowly through the 1970s, and spectacularly in the past decade, the industry has regained a great deal of its status and even come close to recapturing international importance on the scale of the nineteenth century. The context of the industry and its ability to respond to the broad range of possible influences shows why foreign sources of new drugs, as well as foreign exploitation of British developments came to characterize British industry. Far from being a "propensity" to allow advantages to slip away, it was structural characteristics of the industry and the disadvantages of two world wars that mitigated against effective exploitation of new medical developments.

The cases described above, however, are revealing of a great deal about the character of the industry by showing its responses to foreign scientific activities. Never wishing to relinquish its sense of international importance, and at the same time unwilling to institute the structural reforms which were called for at the beginning of the First World War, the industry was forced to respond in a piecemeal manner to each challenge. The consequence slowly brought about a more flexible, better regulated industry, and one more able to respond to the rapidly growing expectations of the increasingly sophisticated medical community.

Notes and References

1. See Jonathan Liebenau, "The British success with penicillin," *Social Studies of Science* 17 (1987): 69. This paper is largely based on archival research in companies and in collections held at the Medical Research Council. This essay includes a reanalysis of a number of detailed studies which the author has published over the past five years.
2. Jonathan Liebenau, "Industrial R&D in pharmaceutical firms in the early twentieth century," *Business History* 24 (1984): 329–346.
3. Jonathan Liebenau, "The international pharmaceutical industry," *Business History* 27 (1987).
4. See Jonathan Liebenau, *Medical Science and Medical Industry, The Formation of the American Pharmaceutical Industry* (London: Macmillan Press; Baltimore: Johns Hopkins University Press, 1987).
5. Jonathan Liebenau, "The MRC and pharmaceuticals development; the case of Insulin," in Joan Austaucher and Linda Bryder, *A History of the MRC* (Oxford: Oxford University Press, 1989).
6. *Lancet* 1 (1923): 814.
7. Editorial, "Therapeutics Substances Bill," *British Medical Journal* 1 (1924): 677.
8. Ibid.
9. MRC Archives, Record Group 1092, "Methods of preparation," p. 15.
10. MRC Archives, Record Group 1092, file VIII "BDH statement," January 1934.
11. Ibid.

12. See Judy Slinn, *A History of May & Baker* (Cheltenham: May & Baker, 1986).
13. This section is largely based on Liebenau, "The British success with penicillin," (n.1).

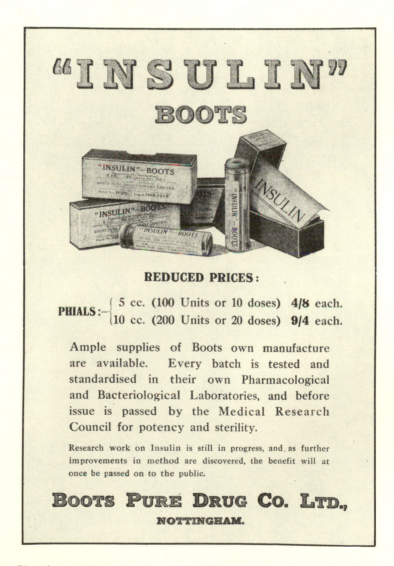

Chemist and Druggist, *June 28, 1924.*